Fundamentals of Word / Information Processing in Business
Concepts in Office Automation

Fundamentals of Word / Information Processing in Business

Concepts in Office Automation

Mary E. Locke

A Reston Book
Prentice-Hall, Inc.
Englewood Cliffs, NJ 07632

Library of Congress Cataloging-in-Publication Data
Locke, Mary E.
 Fundamentals of word/information processing in
business.
 Bibliography: p.
 1. Business—Data processing.   2. Word processing.
I. Title.
HF5548.2.L576   1986   652'.5   85-14418
ISBN 0-8359-2206-5

A Reston Book
Published by Prentice-Hall, Inc.
A Division of Simon & Schuster, Inc.
Englewood Cliffs, NJ 07632

10 9 8 7 6 5 4 3 2 1

PRINTED IN THE UNITED STATES OF AMERICA

Contents

9   Career Opportunities in Information Processing, 181

Glossary of Terms, 195

Appendix, 223

Bibliography, 261

Index, 264

Preface

Fundamentals of Word / Information Processing in Business is the result of a belief shared by many people involved in office automation, that the student studying information processing should be exposed to the realities and concepts of the discipline.

The many vendor photographs and references in the text are evidence of the willingness of manufacturers to assist the student in gaining an awareness of the variety of office automation equipment to be found in business. Though too numerous to mention here, over 75 vendors of information processing and communicating devices were solicited for information incorporated in the text. Of special note is the assistance of Word Processing Enterprises and my former partner, Melody Locke, for the communications documentation found in Chapter 6.

Betty Jo Hathaway, a teacher at Northwest Wisconsin Technical Institute, greatly assisted in the organization of the text as well as encouraging the concepts approach through her early review of the manuscript.

Several educators at Mesa College in Grand Junction, Colorado were involved in the development of this text. I would like to thank Janine Rider, English Instructor, for her guidance and encouragement through the initial writing stages. Special acknowledgement is made of the extensive time given by Tennie Ann Capps, Associate Professor of Office Administration, in reviewing the text, and of her professional advice about the organization of the book.

Significant contributions to Chapter 5 and the Glossary were made by my husband and business partner, Neal Locke,

CDP. His extensive experience in data processing greatly assisted in the sections discussing word and data processing integration. His expertise was also involved in the development of the Glossary which incorporates many data processing terms.

The copyediting of Judy Coughlin gracefully moved the manuscript through the difficult metamorphic stages. Special thanks go to Judy as well as the Reston staff involved in the production of the book. Most importantly, my appreciation to Barbara Lovenvirth, Editor at Reston, who encouraged me to attempt a text related to the concepts of word/information processing.

Mary Locke

Introduction

When today's business student visits the library in search of books about word processing, he or she will be somewhat surprised by the lack of historical documentation of the industry. This observation has a logical basis: the word processing industry has developed at such a rapid pace that as soon as current technology is documented, announcements are made of new or improved capabilities and functions. Office automation consultants find that just keeping abreast of current technology requires more time than is available; administration professionals find that the demand for knowledge of technological advances is a continuing challenge.

It is equally difficult to stay current with the frequency of new manufacturers coming into the marketplace, old established ones who have closed their doors, and the acquisitions of information processing firms by companies desiring to get into high tech.

Illustrating the contemporary quality of these technologies, it was not until the end of the 1970s that we began to see the first dictionary reference to "word processing." The early definitions referred to word processing as the typing of documents and storing them on some type of magnetic media for future revision and use. The scope of word processing has broadened with the incorporation of computerization; no longer could the industry be defined as just typing and processing text. The references to "typing" quickly became "word processing" and then "information processing," as the word processing industry in the 1980s adopted the term to more accurately reflect the multi-capability of these systems. Further, the data processing industry has also adopted *information processing* to reflect its expanded function. The term "information processing" applies in either context, as well as when addressing the numerous intelligent office automation devices that interface with word and data processing. The term is used extensively throughout the book in the context of processing information.

The words "computer" and "microcomputer" are used interchangeably with "word processor" throughout the text as the internal workings of today's word processors are nearly identical with that of a microcomputer. The office worker today may find that he or she will be requested to accomplish a word processing task on a computer or microcomputer; conversely, they may be required to accomplish a data processing task on a word processor. The text often refers to "computer literacy" as a requirement of the office environment. Computer literacy can be defined as having an understanding of the role of computers, as well as a working knowledge of their functions.

Computer literacy, whether incorporated in information processing or data processing, is a key to achieving success in the job market. Understanding microprocessors and their functions, of which word/information processing is a part, is of major importance in business today. The necessity for computer literacy confronts us from many directions, whether a money transaction at a bank walk-up computer terminal, or understanding written messages produced by a computer. Certainly, as we watch television and read articles about the impact of computers on our lives, the message comes through loud and clear that the computer age is upon us. Computers even play a major role in courtrooms to recreate the patterns of accidents. The 1984 Summer Olympics used a comprehensive network of office automation devices to provide communications over a 4500 square mile area. Our daily newspapers are produced on sophisticated terminals supporting state-of-the-art word processing.

Students preparing for entry into the job market of the 1980s will need a vehicle to help usher them into the computerized world of information processing and office automation; a vehicle to help them keep abreast of the pace of technology advancement. In understanding any technology, it is important to understand the early development as a basis of current state-of-the-art capability. This has particular relevance in word processing, as many of the earlier generations of equipment continue to be used, and have a continuing impact in the office.

Today's students have most likely been subjected to computer functions from nursery school through the present. The small computer, with word processing software, is now a part of elementary education and is being incorporated into summer camp programs. In all phases of life, the student is being required to utilize computer facilities, and word/information processing is a major part of that requirement. Schools and universities commonly use terminals in place of the old card catalogue reference facilities in their libraries. Computer services offer document abstract retrieval; the user calls to the screen the possible document resources, makes a selection, and documents choices on either a letter quality or matrix printer. Some colleges now require students to have computers as tools for college studies, the cost being a part of tuition fees.

This book, *Fundamentals of Word / Information Processing in Business,* is designed to introduce you to the concepts of word processing and its fundamental role in business. The book serves to enhance the "hands-on" training you will receive on a given piece of equipment. It documents the evolution of word processing, and the subsequent advances in the industry as a result of computer technology. Further, the text allows the reader to examine the state-of-the-art technology of microprocessor-driven hardware, as well as the programmability of information processing software. The concepts of word processing functions are examined to assist the student in achieving productivity in using word/information processing equipment. The text also addresses how to determine office automation needs of a business through the process of a system analysis, and how to implement the results of such a study. As data, word and information processing often overlap, the glossary of terms at the back of the book deals with basic terminology. Where a term is used in two disciplines with unique meanings, the distinctions are clarified.

In approaching this text, *Fundamentals of Word / Information Processing in Business,* the reader will find that the book has a two-fold purpose: 1) to serve as an introduction to the concepts of word processing functions and capabilities; and, 2) to serve as a guide to incorporate these concepts into the business environment. Thus, the book is both a handbook of hardware and software concepts, and an instructional tool for the design and implementation of information processing in business.

Fundamentals of Word / Information Processing in Business
Concepts in Office Automation

1

Progress of Word/Information Processing

In the 1980s, the United States is rapidly changing from an industrial society to an "information society" as the economy moves from manufacturing to information services. The changes are readily evident in the outward symbols of such a society, as CRT (cathode ray tube) screens and computers pervade our daily lives from the office to the living room. What kind of impact does this type of society have on the traditional office? The business professional? The aspiring entrant to the business world? The reality of the changing business environment demands that the established professional must come to grips with change and retraining; the aspiring professional must be trained in office automation disciplines.

The technology explosion of this information society will bring exciting challenges and opportunities to those who are educated in its disciplines. *Word processing,* in its larger context of information processing, is a major component of the information age. Employment opportunities will be most accessible to those who bring to business and industry a level of knowledge and expertise that will make them valuable assets—in other words, a person who will not require a great deal of additional education to be productive in today's office. The trained person who can also lead and guide others in these disciplines will be particularly valuable.

In the past, major word processing manufacturers, such as Digital Equipment Corporation (DEC), International Business Machines (IBM), and Wang, to name a few, provided operator and supervisor training, as well as advanced courses in system design and implementation. Because of this willingness of manufacturers and vendors to train a client's employees, business and industry did not have to be concerned with the training of entry level personnel. However, in today's marketplace, vendors of word/information processing equipment have found that the cost of educating a client's employees has become prohibitive. Unfortunately, since more and more manufacturers have been forced to discontinue training benefits, word/information processing installations are suffering from a lack of trained entry level personnel. Today's office workers need a thorough knowledge of hardware and office procedures to effectively utilize sophisticated information processing systems.[1] This scarcity of trained personnel has affected both existing and new installations.

The key to success for entrants into the world of office automation is education: education of the past and of the future. Unfortunately, those who are just beginning to gain knowledge of the information age will find this task similar to boarding a fast-moving train; in order to get on board you must get up to speed, as well as have a knowledge of the train. The information age will not come to a convenient stop while everyone gets on board.

As with any discipline, it is important to have an understanding of its evolution to fully comprehend its current state-of-the-art status, and to gain insight into its future. In viewing the word processing industry, this historical knowledge has special significance, as most vendors have built upon previous concepts.

EARLY BEGINNINGS (1950s)

Repetitive Letters: Letters informing a number of people about the same subject matter.

Why do we have word processing? What is word processing? The technology is the result of the old adage, "Necessity is the mother of invention." Shortly after World War II, when the first computers had been favorably received and several vendors were developing their next market entries, the engineers of these systems saw a possible application of paper tape data entry machines in the office support environment. The paper tape "keyboards" simply captured keystrokes by puncturing a paper tape, similar to that of a player piano, but only an inch wide. When read into the computer, the tape served as a method of data entry. As a typing device, it was used mostly for the production of repetitive letters. The standard body of the letter was typed and recorded (punched) on the paper tape,

[1]"Standalone Word Processing Systems," *Datapro Research Reports,* January, 1978.

and then read back through the typewriter tape-reading mechanism. The only typing required was the insertion of the recipients' names and addresses on the letters. This elementary method of reproduction typing significantly increased productivity of secretaries who were required to type the same letter over and over to a long list of names and addresses. The paper tape could not be corrected, however, and after multiple uses it might become torn (sometimes called lacing), requiring the retyping of the tape.

Function: An umbrella term incorporating all automatic capabilities of the equipment.

The major typing requirements of the office had still not been answered, however, with the paper tape applications. What was needed to address the typing needs of the 1960s was a way to capture keystrokes on a medium that would allow for revisions. The development of technology that followed in the word processing industry can be categorized into four distinct generations. Though the word processing equipment is discussed in generations of progress, most of it is still in use today. In reality, though CRT screens and additional memory have been added, the requirement for function has never changed— only the method of providing function.

FIRST GENERATION

Hardware: The physical equipment of a computer system.

Standalone: A single system, containing intelligence and printer.

The first significant strides in the word processing industry were made in 1964 with IBM's first hardware entry, the Magnetic Tape Selectric Typewriter (MT/ST), which incorporated the concept of magnetic storage. Typed characters were captured electronically on magnetic tape media, similar to the tape recorder cassettes used today, though somewhat larger in size. The Selectric typewriter, the first typewriter without a movable carriage, had been well accepted in the office by the early 1960s. By using this familiar keyboard in the MT/ST, IBM introduced the new and revolutionary technology with its well known typewriter. The acceptance of the MT/ST far exceeded IBM's original projections[2] of 6,000 units; about 50,000 systems were installed during the production life of the equipment; it is considered the first standalone word processor.

---

[2]"Educating the User: The Next Challenge," *Words,* April-May, 1984, p. 21.

Keystrokes: Word processing terminology for the typing of characters.

Though the first equipment had minimal text editing capabilities, it represented a major breakthrough in that it was the first effort to "capture" keystrokes electronically. Word processing operators enjoying today's sophisticated software have long taken for granted the simple feature of choosing the character spacing of 10 or 12 characters per inch. However, the addition of this feature provided a level of flexibility the office had never enjoyed, and it had a significant impact on productivity when first introduced. The most important development was the ability to record on magnetic media; documents could be typed, recorded, and revised, and the tape erased and reused. The principal type of medium in this generation was magnetic tape. All functions were established through internal wiring at the time the hardware was manufactured, hence they were "hard-wired." IBM introduced the MT/ST in 1964 and was the only substantial manufacturer in the field until the end of the decade (see Figure 1–1, "Typical System Configurations by Manufacturer").

Figure 1.1.   Typical System Configurations and Representative Manufacturers, 1964–1984.

FIRST GENERATION

Type Hardware	*Type Processing*	*Type Media*	*Media Storage/ Storage Capacity*
MT/ST Selectric	Hardwired	Magnetic Tape	23K chars.
MT/SC Selectric Composer	Hardwired	Magnetic Tape	

Representative Vendors
IBM

SECOND GENERATION

Type Hardware	*Type Processing*	*Type Media*	*Media Storage/ Storage Capacity*
Keyboard Printer Dual Card Console	Hardwired	Magnetic Card	Line Buffer Only
Keyboard Printer Card Console	Hardwired	Magnetic Card	50 lines 8K
Keyboard Printer Cassette Control Console	Hardwired	Tape Cassette	120K chars. N/A

| CRT | Hardwired | Tape Cassette | 140K chars. |

CRT
Printer(s)
  Selectric
  Daisy Wheel

Representative Vendors	*Equipment Identification*	*Media Utilized*
IBM	Mag Card I, II, A	Mag Card
Redactron	Single or Dual	Mag Card or Cassette Tape
Royal	CTS	Cassette Tape
Savin	900 Word Master	Cassette Tape
Ty-Data	Editor 3600	Dual Cassette
Willow	MC-100-200	Dual Cassette Tape or Mag Card
Associates	MT-100-200	
Xerox	800	Dual Cassette Tape or Mag Card

THIRD GENERATION

Type Hardware	*Type Processing*	*Type Media*	*Media Storage/ Memory Size*
Thin Window	Hardwired	Mag Card or Cassette	120/K
Printer Keyboard			None
CRT, Half Page	Hardwired	Cassette, Diskettes	125–300K
Daisy Wheel			None
CRT, 6 Line	Single Disk Drive	8" Diskettes	250/K
Integrated Keyboard	(Hardwired)		8K
Ink Jet Printing			
Print Queuing			
Auto Paper Handling			
Bidirectional Print- ing			
CRT, Half Page	Single/Dual Disk	5¼" Work Diskette	70/K
Integrated Keyboard	(Hardwired)		32K
Shared Printing			
CRT, Full Page	Dual Diskette	8" Work Diskette	300/K
Diskette			16K

Representative Vendors	*Equipment Identification*	*Media Utilized*
CPT	8000	Disk
IBM	OS/6	Disk
Lanier*	No Problem	Disk
Lexitron**	920, 940, 1000 series	Tape
Micom (Philips)	2000	Disk
Q1	Q1/LMC	Disk
Redactron	Redactor II	Tape
Wang	1222, WP 10A	Disk
Xerox	850 Page Display	Disk

* Merged with Harris, 1983
** Discontinued marketing in May, 1984

Figure 1.1.   (*continued*)

SHARED-LOGIC, 1973–1979

Type Hardware	*Number of Terminals*	*Type Media*	*Memory Size*
Minicomputer	2–32	1 to 4 Discs	4K–128K
		Hard Disk	
		Floppy Diskettes for	
		Archiving	

Representative Vendors	*Equipment Identification*	*Media Utilized*
Computek	Accutext Barrister	1–8 Discs
Digital Equipment	WS Series 102, 200	1–8 Discs &
Corp.	WP 11	Diskettes
Four Phase	ForeWord	Disc
ICS	Wordsystem 112	1–4 Discs
LCS	Computext	1–4 Discs, Diskettes
Xerox	Daconics	1–4 Discs

FOURTH GENERATION

Type Hardware	*Type Capability*	*Type Media*	*Media Storage/ Memory Size*
Display	Single/Dual Disk	Diskettes	130 pages to
Detached Keyboard	Single/Dual Density		350 pages
Electronics Module			
Diskette Unit		Hard Disk Available	128/k–448K
Printer Sharing		for Increased Storage	
(1–4 terminals)	Data Processing (DP)		
Communications	Operating Systems		
Interface	DP Software		

*Representative Vendors**	*Equipment Identification*	*Media Utilized*	*Possible Configurations*
A.B. Dick	Magna Series	5¼″ & 8″ Diskettes	
		Hard Disk Option	Standalones or
			Multistation
			Computer Operating System Option
Burroughs	OFIS Series	5¼″ Diskettes	Standalone or
		Hard Disk	Multistation
			Compatible Microcomputers
Compucorp	700 Series	5¼″ Diskettes	Standalones
		Hard Disk Option	Network for Sharing
			Computer Operating System Option
CPT	8500 Series	8″ Diskettes	Standalones
	Phoenix	Hard Disk Option	Network for Sharing
			Computer Operating System Option

DEC	DECmate II	5¼" Diskettes	Integrated WP/DP
Exxon Office Systems	500 & 750 Series	5¼" Diskettes	Standalones and Shared
		Hard Disk Option	Logic
			Compatible Microcomputers
IBM	Displaywriter	8" Diskettes	Standalones; Shared Printers
			Network for Sharing
			Computer Operating System Option
	5520 System	Hard Disk	Shared Logic
Lanier	Business Processor	5¼" Diskettes	Standalone;
			Network for Sharing
			Computer Operating System Option
NBI	OASys 4000 Series	8" Diskettes	Standalone; shared resource
			Computer Operating System Option
	System 8 & 64	Hard Disk	Integrated Processing
NEC	Astra Series	Hard Disk	Up to 16 stations; Integrated WP/DP
Sony	Series 35	3.5" Diskettes	Standalone;
		2–4 Disk Drives	Shared Printers
			Computer Operating System Option
Syntrex	Aquarius	5¼" Diskettes	Shared Logic
	Gemini	Hard Disk	Computer Operating System Option
Wang	Office Assistant	5¼" Diskettes	Standalone
			Computer Operating System Option
	OIS 40 and 50	Floppy Diskettes and	Standalone;
		Hard Disk	Shared Printers
	Alliance 250	Hard Disk	Multiterminal, Shared Logic
Xerox	860 Information Processor	8" Diskettes	Shared Printers
			Network for Sharing
			Computer Operating System Option

* Information supplied by vendors

SECOND GENERATION

The word processing industry during the next generation, 1969 through 1972, was for the most part dominated by IBM with the introduction of the Mag Card Selectric Typewriter. The use of magnetic cards (mag cards) as recording media was significant in that recording of a document was not hindered by the medium's size. The concept of "page to card," plus no limitations on media size, was found to be a logical step and was readily accepted by operators.

The second generation saw a number of new manufacturers enter the word processing industry with a variety of magnetic card and magnetic cassette tape equipment. Though some types of equipment were more sophisticated than others,

Figure 1-2   IBM Magnetic Card Selectric Typewriter II. (*Courtesy IBM Corporation.*)

the most important advances included improved revision capability, increased storage capacity at lower cost, and additional functions. IBM introduced the innovative concept of internal memory to allow text to be manipulated prior to storing on magnetic media or during revision. The major feature of the IBM Mag Card II (see Figure 1–2) allowed this internal memory to be divided, which created a main and an alternate memory. This capability introduced the function of MERGE, allowing variable information to be merged into a basic or standard document. Neither of these two concepts were duplicated by any other vendor in this generation, as all other vendors used direct-key-to-media-storage (recording) concepts. Additional basic functions that appeared in this generation were automatic centering, multiple word underscore, the recording of tab stops, and decimal tab.

Dual mag card or tape machines of this era used the dual media to accomplish a merge. During a revision process, the new version of the document was immediately transferred to the second magnetic card or tape.

THIRD GENERATION

In the third generation, 1973–1979, the majority of dedicated word processing equipment continued to utilize circuit boards (hard-wired) for function capability. By the mid 1970s most vendors were offering disk technology, which incorporated the first use of visual displays or CRTs. The Lexitron VT–900 Series was the first CRT-based word processor; the fourth model produced is displayed at the Smithsonian Institution.[3] Rapid technology advancements occurred during the period, swelling the number of word processing companies well into the hundreds. Typical of this generation was the IBM OS/6, which used an eight-inch floppy disk, shown in Figure 1–3, and the CPT model 4200, which used a cassette for the recording medium, as shown in Figure 1–4.

---

[3]Letter received from Rathon Data Systems Company, Norwood, MA, 27 Feb., 1984.

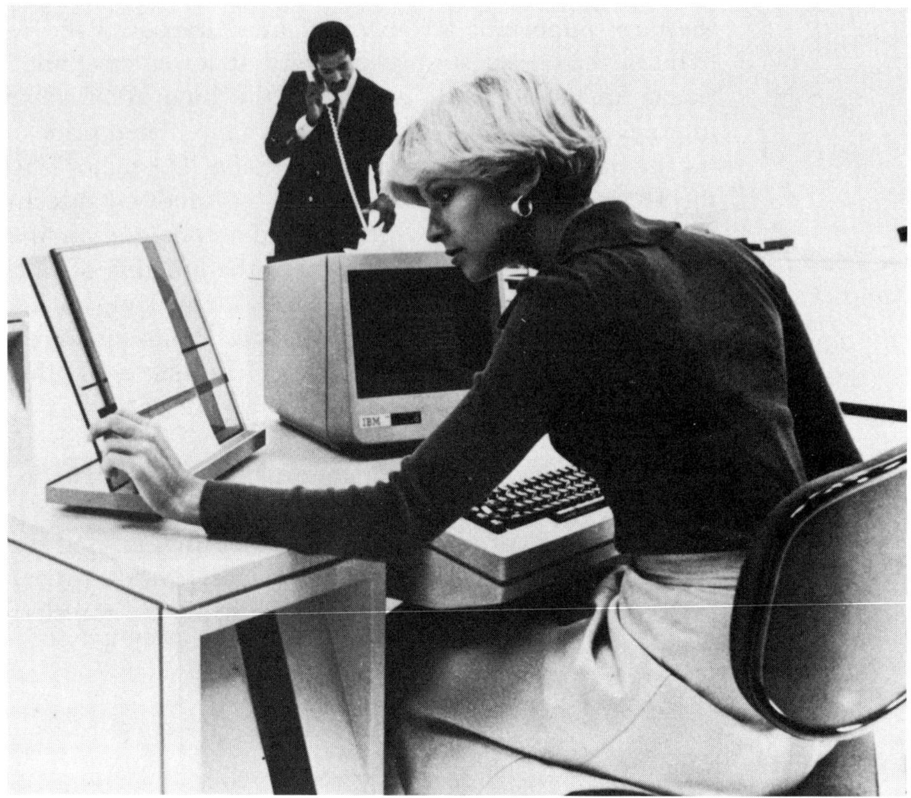

Figure 1-3 IBM OS/6–450. (*Courtesy IBM Corporation.*)

New Technology

Significant changes in technology occurred during the last half of the 1970s. The invention of the flexible disk drive and the subsequent disk technology of menu driven systems, CRTs, daisy wheel, ink jet, laser printers, and records and list processing drastically changed the world of word processing during this period. Though most of the technology was still considered to be hard-wired, the end of the period saw the introduction of microprocessor-based word processing. The systems were still basically standalone, sharing a printer, or they were shared-logic (see below), multistation configurations. Most important to this era was that the operator could see on the screen what was being typed, as well as what had been recorded previously.

Figure 1-4   CPT Model 4200. (*Courtesy CPT Corporation.*)

Cursor keys allowed the operator to find the point of any requested revisions and to mark text to be moved or copied. The era of sophisticated text editing had arrived; complemented by multiple pitch and font printing, including right hand justification, records and list processing and tailored communications, the era of information processing at the word processing work station was born.

Shared-Logic Systems

As with the original effort to capture keystrokes, the need to share information brought the concept of shared-logic systems into the marketplace. Standalone hardware was very expensive during this period, as were minicomputers; however, large legal and accounting firms saw the need to share common information not available in standalone systems. In most cases, these early systems were provided by the existing mainframe computer firms. Word processing software written for shared-logic systems was not quite as sophisticated as on standalones, but the ability to connect multiple terminals to a common central computer for storage and standard document sharing definitely had a demand. Xerox Corporation bought the existing technology of a California entrepreneur company, Daconics, during this period, and Xerox pioneered the way for shared-logic systems in the word processing industry.

FOURTH GENERATION

Microprocessor: Central component in a small computer where processing takes place.

Diskette: External storage media in the form of a flexible disk in a paper-like container.

When word processing hardware manufacturers began using the microprocessor (silicon chip) in the early 1980s, it marked the distinct birth of the fourth generation of information processing, as memory was no longer dependent upon extensive printed circuit boards as in previous generations. Software offered increased capabilities, as they were now provided for through an external diskette containing the particular word processing program. Providing additional functions became a contest of programmers' imaginations. The contest between hardware manufacturers produced numerous new "gimmicks" that quickly became requirements and then standards. Such capabilities as spelling checks, four function math, stored keystrokes and glossaries, multi-string searches, conditional text in merge functions, and continuous operator "help screens" are but a few of the innovations in the past few years (discussed further in Chapter 2).

Few people in the business world today have not heard of, or been affected by, the microcomputer; this generation of hardware is most notably identified by the incorporation of the microprocessor (silicon chip) and external programming (software). Most certainly, information processing has come of age. The capability, functionality, and scope of today's word processor has made it a vital component of information processing. Manufacturers have chosen a variety of "internal processors" for information processing and microcomputer systems: the

Intel 8086 and 8088; the Motorola 68000, and the Z–80 series, to name a few (discussed in Chapter 2).

These same processors are found in today's microcomputers. The major difference in hardware between a dedicated word processor and a microcomputer is the keyboard. Each keyboard has function keys that directly relate to the particular discipline. However, word processors can perform data processing applications normally associated with computers, just as microcomputers can perform word processing functions. Each has its own software and appropriate operating system. As you will learn in Chapter 3, the equipment decision is dictated by the major purpose of the business or department personnel using the equipment.

Figure 1-5   NBI 4000S. (*Courtesy NBI Corporation.*)

Software: Programming or programs for the computer hardware.

Ergonomic Design: Design takes human working environment into consideration.

The emphasis of function for this generation is on software and sharing of resources. Ideally, procuring new hardware should be a thing of the past as new function is usually supplied through upgrades in software. However, two or three years into this generation of hardware, manufacturers continued to introduce new, more "ergonomically designed" machines. The next hardware emphasis was on "small footprints"—the amount of space a machine occupies on a desk—tiltable screens, and moveable, detached keyboards. A representative fourth generation standalone system is the NBI OASys 4000S (see Figure 1–5). The work-station fits on a 19–inch area, featuring an ergonomically designed 25-line operator-adjustable table display with anti-glare screen, the new

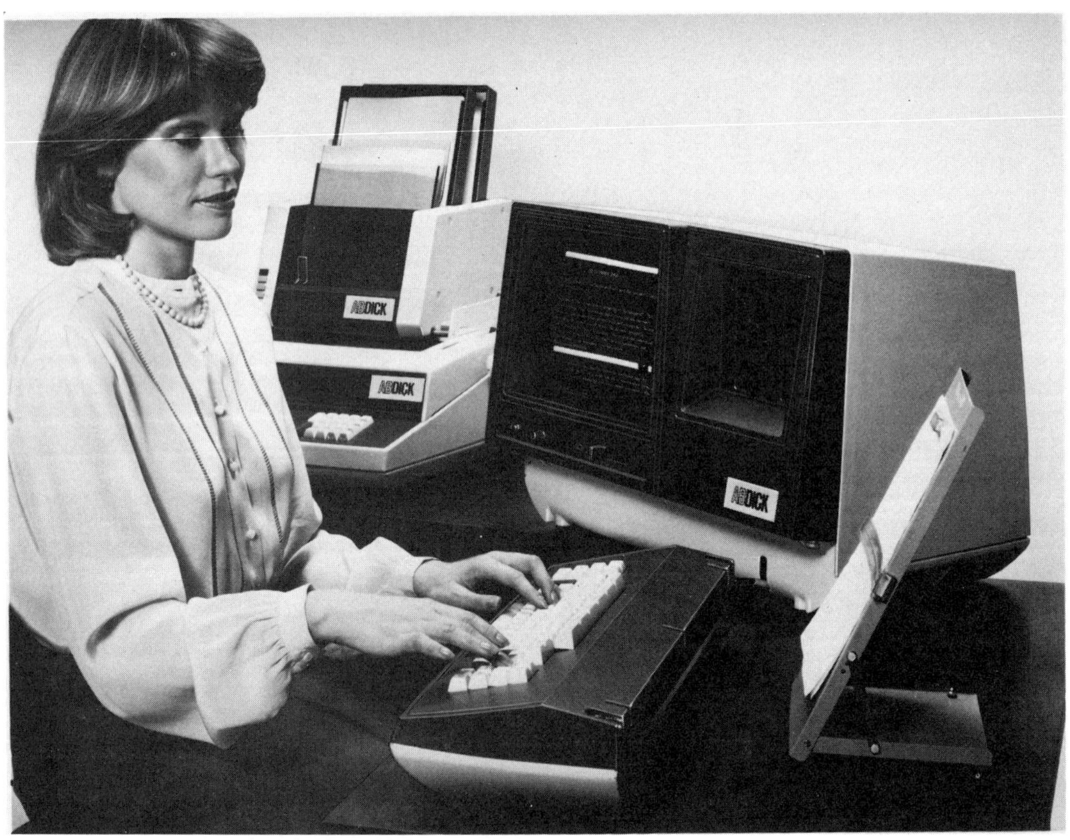

Figure 1-6 AB Dick Magna III. (*Courtesy AB Dick Corporation.*)

low-profile detached keyboard, and eight-inch disk drives for single, dual, or quad density diskettes.

Clustered Concept: Group of standalones which share a common printer.

Improved software programs and operating systems have brought new function to information processing. The current generation provides for configuration options—for example, using a system as an intelligent standalone or in a clustered concept—where data communcations capability provides for the sharing of data. The AB Dick Magna III System (see Figure 1–6) configures a raised keyboard and 5½-inch dual density disk drive and uses a distributed intelligence technology. Each component has its own microprocessor that can perform a number of functions at the same time.

Figure 1-7   Digital Equipment Corporation DECmate II. (*Courtesy Digital Equipment Corporation.*)

Operating Systems:
Software which con-
trols hardware func-
tions of a computer.

Third Party Vendors:
Firms that write soft-
ware for existing
hardware.

As we have discussed before, most information processing systems also support data processing through a number of operating systems. Those most popularly supported are CP/M, MSDOS, Unix or UCSD. Digital Equipment Corporation's DECmate Office Workstation uses DECmate word processing software, Easycom communications, list processing, sort and math, and Digital Research's CP/M (Version 2.0), shown in Figure 1–7. A vast number of data processing programs are available from third party vendors for information processors; some vendors feature integrated processing; that is, material can be exchanged between data processing and information processing programs. These concepts are further supported through the addition of "windows" allowing the user to view two different "files" at one time for possible combining into text, graphics, or data processing applications.

FIFTH GENERATION

Though the fifth generation of information processing hardware and software is imminent, industry prophets are somewhat divided as to the direction it will take. The advent of technology to come is discussed further in Chapter 2.

DISCUSSION QUESTIONS

1. What advantages did magnetic tape have over paper tape as a recording medium?
2. How has OA (office automation) affected older established white collar workers?
3. Define internal memory.
4. Differentiate the four generations of word processing evolution.
5. How does the use of a CRT display increase operator productivity?
6. How do shared-logic systems differ from standalones?
7. What is the primary distinction in hardware between a microcomputer and a word processor?

2

Evaluating Word/Information Processing Hardware and Software

The de facto standards that have been established for word processing have come about through a process of competing manufacturers and vendors providing new functions and, as a consequence, users becoming accustomed to these new functions and accepting them as standards and/or requirements.

This continuing demand for new and improved capability can be compared to what we expect in our television viewing. Can you imagine how unhappy we would be if some television broadcasters were capable of providing "instant replay" in football games and others were not? What was considered state-of-the-art yesterday is not acceptable today; the latest gimmick today may become tomorrow's standard. This constant upward mobility in the demand for improved and new features has ushered the industry along at a rapid pace, making analysis of features and systems a monumental task. However, the key to evaluation lies in the ability of the particular feature to increase productivity.

Not only have new features and functions become de facto standards, but existing ones have been upgraded to increase productivity. An example of this type of upgrade is underscoring groups of words, one of the earliest de facto standards. In early word processors, in order to underscore more than one word, the operator placed required spaces (a code key in combination with the space bar) between words and a word underscore instruction at the end of the phrase or group of words. This concept was time consuming and awkward. Furthermore, the editing function was inhibited, as the intelligence of the system read the underscored text as a single word. Before the editing could be accomplished with this technology, all of the required spaces had to be deleted.

Improved hardware and software of the fourth generation introduced "begin underscore" and "end underscore" function keys. In other words, now the operator simply inserts an instruction to underscore, types the material to be underscored at burst speed, and concludes with an end instruction. Whole paragraphs or pages can be underscored with only two coded strokes. In addition, the text between the underscore instructions can be edited through additions or deletions without interrupting the line ending adjustments. This evolutionary change in a traditional function is a marked improvement over earlier methods, has increased productivity, and has become an integral part of word processing de facto standards.

Concepts: The approach taken to achieve a particular function or feature.

In this chapter, de facto standards of the "fourth generation" hardware and software concepts are examined. Their impact on word and records processing are measured to provide an understanding of the industry and the uniqueness of word processing. Those standards that are inherent to either the standalone or shared-logic environments exclusively will be noted; otherwise, the de facto standards are assumed to be applicable to all dedicated word processing systems.

MENU-DRIVEN SYSTEMS

The concept by which fourth generation word and data processing software provides choices of work to be done is accomplished through a series of screens, called *menus.* Since software vendors incorporate their own particular approaches to these menus, their use is universal and the approaches are not addressed in the discussion of de facto standards.

Manufacturers of word processing hardware and software differ in their approach to providing the de facto standards. This becomes even more apparent in the word processing software written for microcomputers, discussed in greater detail in Chapter 3.

In the following sections, the established de facto standards of program software and machine hardware are described and evaluated. You will be able to compare the standard functions and features with the particular equipment you are currently training on or one that you are familiar with in your past experience.

EVALUATING DE FACTO SOFTWARE STANDARDS

Text Processing Functions

AUTO WORD WRAP

Auto word wrap allows a typist to continue typing without being concerned about carriage returning. Since burst typing speed is known to be three to four times faster than that possible if an operator has to be concerned with line endings, this function rates high in the increased productivity evaluation. Although it causes some disorientation during the revision cycle, as the hard copy no longer looks like the screen, the feature's strong points far outweigh any negative aspects (a discussion of the negative aspect during communications is found in Chapter 6).

INSERT MODE

Systems vary considerably on how the inserting of material can be accomplished during the editing process.

- The preferred approach allows for the insert mode to be active in all stages of keyboarding. In this instance, the concept allows for inserts to be made at any time, whether during the initial keyboarding or during the editing stage.

- Another insert concept allows for the insert mode to be active only during the original keyboarding. However, during the edit phase the cursor must be placed at the position of the insert, and a "code insert" instruction must be given. Once the inserted material has been typed, a "code insert" instruction concludes the process.

- Still another concept requires that a "code insert" instruction be given, and a blank line or space opens up splitting the existing text on the screen. The insert is typed, followed by another coded instruction to end the insert. The existing text then closes up around the inserted text.

- Insert/Replace. This feature allows the keyboarder to simply type the insert over existing unwanted text. The feature is useful when there is a great deal of text to be deleted and added. The new words replace the unwanted text as the insertion progresses.

The numerous concepts used in providing the insert function in word processing require that users carefully analyze their work. Those business firms or users who tend to have lengthy projects that are frequently edited should carefully examine which concept would be the most productive.

DELETE

Though the ability to delete characters, words, lines, and paragraphs was one of the original word processing capabilities, the method or approach varies considerably between manufacturers. The concept of cursor movement is tied very closely to the manner in which material is deleted. If a particular system can cursor or advance through the text by character, word, sentence, paragraph, and page, the delete function will most likely be provided for in the same increments.

The delete function should be a two part process: First, the area to be deleted should be highlighted, and second, the delete function should actually be carried out. Some systems provide an "electronic wastebasket" concept where all deleted material resides. This feature is invaluable for authors who can't make up their minds, as retrieving the deleted material is accomplished with relative ease. Regardless of the approach, DELETE should preferably be accomplished by a dedicated function key on the keyboard, not through a menu option (see list under the subject "Function Keys" listed below).

CURSOR MOVEMENT

Full cursor movement is the ability to move the cursor in six directions, as well as a command capability to instruct the cursor to move by word, sentence or paragraph. This flexibility is important to the editing phase of word processing. Some systems have limitations in that the cursor either moves by one position at a time, or one line at a time; thus the sentence and paragraph access are not provided. The lack of full cursor movement can constrict productivity somewhat in the MOVE and COPY functions discussed below.

MOVE

"MOVE" is the transferring of material from one place to another and deleting it from its original location. The highlighting of text to be moved provided in the fourth generation greatly enhances the moving of material. Most systems highlight this text by the use of an outstanding color or a shading of the background color. As in the discussion of INSERT concepts, the MOVE function is also restricted by the concepts of the software.

- The move process is sometimes restricted by the number of pages that can be moved at one time. This usually results when pages are stored by the system as "hard pages." This is often referred to as a "page-oriented" system.
- Some systems do not provide for a "temporary" depository for text, such as a glossary or phrasing function (see Glossary and Phrasing). When undertaking complicated text editing, the lack of such a temporary facility for depositing or moving text is considered unproductive. The best of both worlds would allow for a temporary depositing of text, such as a glossary or phrase function, and then a deletion of that temporary text once it is permanently moved.

COPY

"COPY" is the same as "MOVE" except that the material is not deleted from its original location. The COPY function should have the same flexibility as the move function. For often repeated text, formats, chart outlines, etc., the glossary or phrase concept is a plus here, too.

GLOBAL SEARCH AND REPLACE

This feature allows a system to search for repeated occurrences of words or phrases requiring change and causes the automatic replacement with the new text. So important is this function to productivity that the only difference in the way vendors treat this de facto standard is in how many searches can take place at one time. Fairly standard approaches are to offer five single word or phrase search and replacements at one pass. Complementary to this function is the ability to monitor the process or have it accomplished automatically according to the operator's wishes.

GLOSSARY AND PHRASING

The concept of storing temporary or often used material for future insertion, this feature is one of the most logical functions on the de facto list. In essence, these features give the ability to either move text to a temporary "memory" or to purposely record often-used text that can be easily recalled for insertion. The only difference is the terminology used in the particular hardware model. The practical applications of this feature are limitless in document production.

SCREEN PROMPTS

At today's level of software, whether targeted at the experienced or inexperienced operator, the user has the right to expect "user-friendly" interaction with a program. For example, when an operator inadvertently presses the "ENTER" key instead of the "END" key to conclude a function, user-friendly software should "prompt" the operator of the incorrect function, as well as providing prompts to perform the correct function. Some of today's more innovative software, such as the IBM Displaywriter Textpack 4, allows the operator to bypass instruction prompts once he or she becomes proficient with the system.

FUNCTION KEYS

It is difficult to overestimate the value of function keys for quality word processing; they are inherent to the concept of productivity. In addition to the active cursor keys previously discussed, the function keys for BACKSPACE DELETE, FIND, GO TO, DELETE, MOVE, COPY, GET, and GLOBAL SEARCH should be present. If the software requires that the function of INSERT must be activated, that function should preferably be represented by a dedicated key.

Additional function keys that assist in productivity are

SPELL, PRINT, LINE DELETE, WORD DELETE, and CHARACTER DELETE (see Hardware Standards for function keyboard location).

PAGINATION

Pagination is the term applied to the automatic changing of page endings when material has been added or deleted. This feature is important in the editing stages when the addition of new material forces changes in page length. Software differs relative to the concept of the vendor, i.e., page-oriented systems paginate as an operator function, whereas document-oriented systems paginate as an automatic function. As the operation can be time consuming, it is beneficial to have pagination and repagination combined with another function, such as a spelling check or hyphenation pass.

SPELLING VERIFICATION

There is significant variation in concept between vendors who provide spelling verification. For example, the CPT systems provide instant notice to operators by sounding a tone when a word is incorrectly typed (see Figure 2–1). In other systems, the operator is prompted of misspelled words through a manual or automatic highlighting procedure. Spelling dictionaries have a range in size varying from 5,000 to 100,000 words. The IBM Displaywriter Textpack 6 (see Figure 2–2), for example, has 100,000 words in its spell check. If the user wishes to utilize this function extensively, a minimum size spelling dictionary would fall at the 50,000 word level. The supplemental dictionary feature allows the user to add the most often used, industry-oriented words. The minimum standard for supplemental dictionaries should allow the addition of 2,000 words.

CENTERING

Mnemonic: A coding scheme where the first letter of a function represents the keyboard command.

The CENTER function allows words and sentences to be centered in a page or over a column. Another original de facto standard, some systems offer a function key for centering. However, following the mnemonic concept, the centering function is most commonly accomplished by use of a code key in conjunction with the letter "C." Improved software also offers automatic centering in the edit and underscore mode.

Figure 2-1   CPT Phoenix™ System. (*Courtesy CPT Corporation.*)

BOLDFACE

Boldface print is accomplished by two different methods, depending upon the manufacturer. One method provides for the characters to be printed a second time just slightly to the right of the first character. The second method causes the words to be typed a second time directly on top of the original printing. One of the most widely adopted standards, boldface printing contributes cosmetically to a finished document. Some systems show the boldface print on the screen, while others show bold instructions on the screen.

RIGHTHAND JUSTIFICATION

Righthand-justified is the term applied to the alignment of text down the right margin. This is considered fundamental to any

Figure 2-2   IBM Displaywriter. (*Courtesy IBM Corporation.*)

information processing standalone or shared-logic system. The quality of print is somewhat dependent upon the choice of printer; righthand justification and proportional printing are not always offered on the same printer (see the section on Printer Hardware later in this chapter).

MATH IN TEXT

This feature allows the operator to add, subtract, multiply, or divide within columns or row of figures, and provides a welcome alternative to time-consuming proofing, as well as relieving the stress of typing numbers. The operator has confidence that incorrect numbers will be found by the system instead of by the originator. With software allowing mathematical functions to be stored on the disk, any revision passes are guaranteed to produce perfect results.

AUTO COLUMN LAYOUT

Anyone who has ever been confronted with the typing of a multi-column budget, for example, complete with descriptions of years passed and projections of years yet to come, can certainly appreciate this addition to the de facto standards list. Not only does the function allow for the automatic arranging of columns across a page, but the ability to move columns is usually present also. This function has obvious applicability in updating information from one year to the next. For example, the column that represented the current year's budget will be moved next year to the column headed "last year's budget." No longer does an operator have to fret about the originator who can't make up his or her mind how a budget should be presented, e.g., "Should we present last year's figures first or this year's?"

MULTI-COLUMN TEXT

Many companies write their own in-house newsletters or provide multi-column text to a printer. The ability to set up righthand justified multi-columns automatically is available on many systems today. Some systems have software sophisticated enough to show multi-columns on the screen.

TAB FUNCTION(S)

The recording of tab functions became a reality in the third generation and has been expanded in the fourth. Most systems now allow material to be aligned around left flush tabs, as well as right flush, decimal, comma, and center tabs. If an accounting firm were planning to acquire a word processor, the features of decimal and comma tabs would be of great interest.

CONTROL OF FORMAT

The system should allow an unlimited number of format changes within a document. These include the ability to change vertical spacing, indent level, righthand justification, and type style. As an example, technical documents using numerous Greek symbols in multiple formulas require constant format changes on a page. This type of document also incorporates the use of indented paragraphs, which places further demand on this function. Systems that do not allow for unlimited format decisions will cause document production difficulties and should be avoided.

PAGE NUMBERING

Primary to efficient word processing, page numbering has long been a de facto standard. Preferably, the feature should allow numbering to take place at the top or bottom of a page, as well as at either side of the page.

HEADERS AND FOOTERS

Documents often require page numbering within a descriptive heading, or a chapter title at the top or bottom of a page. The trend is for dedicated word processors to have this feature; however, it is often lacking in word processing software for microcomputers. Although important, this feature may be sacrificed in the effort to keep costs down.

FOOTNOTE TRAVEL

Though more applicable to writers of scientific and technical documentation, the ability to type footnotes and retain the integrity of their location, regardless of text revisions and editing, is extremely productive for the author and the keyboarder. This function was quickly accepted as a de facto standard.

AUTOMATIC OUTLINING

This feature allows for Roman and Arabic levels, as well as alphabetic characters, to be automatically generated in text at the request of the operator. Though not necessarily a de facto standard, the feature is becoming more popular and currently represents feature competition among vendors. CPT, NBI and IBM, for example, currently offer the automatic outlining function, found very useful by firms who produce a great many manuals.

SCREEN-VISIBLE IMBEDDED CODES

Screen-visible imbedded format commands can greatly enhance one's ability to edit. Without this feature, the benefits of using a CRT screen in preparation of documents is diminished. Standardization among vendors for these codes has yet to occur; one system may use a caret (ˆ) symbol for a hyphen and another a star (*) for the same purpose. In either case, an operator needs to know where an imbedded code is and what it means. Most systems also prompt the operator somewhere on the screen as to the meaning of the code.

SIMULTANEOUS INPUT, EDITING, AND PRINTING

This feature enables the printing of one document while allowing another to be created or edited. Adopted as a standard to promote productivity, simultaneous input/editing and printing are readily found in fourth generation word processing equipment. However, this feature is often lacking on microcomputer word processing software.

AUTOMATIC DISK INDEX

Often the contents of a disk need to be examined. Since documents or projects are all given names, the importance of having a list to review quickly becomes apparent. Most systems create this index automatically; however, a few vendors still require the operator to input the information. The de facto standard suggests that this index creation be automatic. Systems vary as to the information found in the index, such as percentage of disk space available, additional description of the document stored, time and date document entered and last used, etc.

Records Processing Functions

The ability of dedicated word processing equipment to perform records processing provides the user with the added dimension of information processing; unfortunately, all too few users are aware of a system's ability to serve as an office organizer and record keeper. By definition, records processing allows a file of information to be created; for example, a compilation of regional sales. This compilation might include the name of the region, the salesperson, the product sold, the price of the product, and the commission of the salesperson. Each individual bit of information is referred to as a "field," and all of the fields relating to one sale are called a "record." The entire set of records pertaining to a project is called a "file." Although industry and office function applications of records processing is discussed in Chapter 3, the various outputs and standard functions of records processing are discussed in the following section.

LIST AND REPORT PROCESSING

Many lists need to be kept current in an office environment. Most often these lists are kept for mailing purposes, but they may also be used for updating information on employees, telephone directories, inventory, or customers.

Ascending/Descending: Going up or down in order

List processing involves using all or part of the information in a file to create specialized lists or reports. For example, when the sales department needs a list of all employees and there is no need to include any other fields of information, list processing uses a sort function to search through the file and create a listing of the pertinent information requested. In addition to drawing out the information desired, list processing can sort and output (print) the list in a particular order, such as by years of longest employment and in alphabetcial order within those years. The sort function should allow for the alpha or numeric, as well as for ascending or descending order. Four function math caculations within reports, such as length of employment times a constant for retirement pay information, is now considered a necessary standard.

MERGE FILE/TEXT

Merging files of information with text not only increases productivity, but allows greater use of previously stored lists with standard text documents. Repetitive letters, wills, contracts, and forms all use the merge file/text function. The records processing feature provides for the automatic merging of the variable information in files with the constant information in documents. The four-function math capability can also be active in the merge file/text function. Some systems send the merged information directly to the printer, while others merge the information on a diskette or disk, with the operator sending it to the printer; no one concept is necessarily better than the other, though incorporating the latter method allows the operator to use the system for additional production. It is important to remember that during the merge to print function, the processor is searching and organizing information and does not allow the user to proceed until the merge is completed. The greatest productivity occurs when merges are performed directly to disk with printing occurring after the merge is complete. Still other vendors provide the option of viewing merged documents on a CRT before they are printed.

SEARCH AND COUNT

Often, information is requested but a printout is not required. In the search function, information can be requested, such as how many employees are at a certain location. The operator queries a certain field, in this case the location field, and asks the system to count and display the answer. Additional applications of this function are discussed in the Applications section.

COMMUNICATIONS

Communications capability is listed here more for the important role it plays in office procedures than as a standard. Large computers and dedicated word processing equipment have used communications as a method of inputting and retrieving information for a good many years. Bringing the microcomputer into the office to serve as a professional work station has created a need for these machines to "talk to each other," and to share and send information to one another. Telecommunication and office automation vendors, in an effort to provide this capability, have introduced several technologies for this type of communication (a fuller discussion of communications is found in Chapter 6).

OPTICAL CHARACTER READING

OCR equipment is most likely to be found in word processing environments where Selectric typewriters are used for original keyboarding. The scanning capability of the OCR equipment "reads" the typed characters and converts them into digital signals. These digital signals are then communicated to the diskette or disk of the word processor. Figure 2–3 displays the Sperry Word Processing Workstation with an attached OCR unit. Another major use for this technology is in conjunction with media conversion, as described in Chapter 7. Once again,

Figure 2-3   Sperry Model 30 Desk Station. (*Courtesy Sperry Corporation Computer Systems.*)

this technology is listed here in the area of standards because of the vital role it plays as an input device.

GRAPHICS

Graphics is the ability to chart and graph statistical information and is a relatively new function for dedicated word processing equipment. Though the lines in charts and graphs are currently printed only horizontally or vertically, the printers that support the major word processing vendors do provide shadings of print to enhance graphics printout.

One of the most utilitarian functions of graphics has been the professional creation of organization charts. The ability to draw a given size square, copy it numerous times, and have the spacing between squares automatically performed has made this capability most desirable. Additional touches have been added by vendors, making de facto standards difficult to establish.

Few standards have been established in this function; Philips Information Systems has provided graphics capability for an extensive period of time. IBM Displaywriter creates four kinds of charts (bar, line, pie, and free form), and calculates the proportions through the math function included in Textpack 4 and 6. NBI offers graphics in their clustered OASys 2000 personal computing work station (see Figure 2–4). Each dot on the

Figure 2-4 NBI 2000 PC. (*Courtesy NBI Corporation.*)

display is individually addressed. The OASys 2000 can also access information stored in host computers through asynchronous or bisynchronous communication, and is IBM 3270 compatible.

DATA PROCESSING OPERATING SYSTEMS

Though data processing capability on word processing hardware is not a de facto standard at this time, most standalones and some shared-logic systems can be used for data processing applications. As a general rule, fourth generation word processing equipment uses the same internal processors as do microcomputers, such as Intel 8086, Motorola 68000 or Zilog 8000 series chips (microprocessors). Consequently, the only requirement needed to accomplish data processing is the presence of an operating system (see Chapter 5 for a full discussion) and appropriate applications software. Manufacturers have chosen to issue these products under their own names or have "blessed" outside vendors' products.

Integrated Processing: The ability to combine the results of word and data processing programs.

Information processing forecasters predict that by 1990 the intelligent work stations, such as word processors, microcomputers, and shared-logic systems, will all have integrated processing. This direction has a few technology hurdles to scale, but forecasters believe it is the path of the future. Forecasters are doing just that: forecasting. The reality of the office in the 80s is dealing with the problem of achieving more with less. If a given piece of hardware can accomplish all tasks, even though it requires different software to achieve this goal, then business will choose this cost-saving direction.

SUMMARY

In summary, de facto standards for word processing are judged by two major concepts:

- The standard reflects a realistic function that is required in office automation.
- The standard promotes increased productivity and incorporates recognized word processing concepts.

The software available for today's word processing equipment places very powerful function capability at the keyboard. The professional in the information processing field recognizes and uses the total function availability. This recognition will most likely be called upon at some point in a career, particularly during the period when a systems design analysis is being conducted, as discussed in Chapter 7. The professional analyst recognizes the presence of de facto standards and incorporates them to continually increase productivity and improve the quality of procedures.

EVALUATING DE FACTO HARDWARE STANDARDS

Standards for hardware have been established primarily by the manufacturing community, though recent ergonomic trends have dictated certain priorities. Productivity is directly influenced by hardware, as well as software features and functions.

Ergonomics: Development of hardware conducive to human interface.

The reduction in station costs attributed to printer sharing is important to a standalone environment and is considered to be a de facto standard (see Figure 2–5, Exxon 520 Systems sharing desktop ink-jet printer).

The layout of function keys also plays a role in attaining productivity goals. Keyboards that require an operator to memorize blank or numerical key positions in order to call up functions hamper productivity. All function keys should be logically placed on a keyboard with as little opportunity for operator error as possible.

CRT PHYSICAL STANDARDS

The advent of the CRT made physical standards an issue. Prior to that time, standalone equipment generally followed the concept of an electronic typewriter with either a table-top tape drive or a floor-model console. The first CRT models were large, floor-based, console and printer configurations, requiring a great deal of floor space. The microprocessor generation, oriented to the desk top, has undergone several modifications since its first appearance.

Figure 2-5   Exxon System 520. (Note: In February, 1985, Exxon Office Systems, U.S.A., was purchased by the Harris Lanier Corporation. They will continue to service Exxon Office Systems but no new equipment or software will be manufactured under that name.)

Footprint: The amount of desk space required for CRT unit.

The depth of the CRT and keyboard combined, the "footprint," has been modified by many vendors in order to allow the equipment to fit on traditional office furniture; thus, an industry-oriented de facto standard has evolved. However, a great many vendors have chosen not to consider this problem and the acquisition of new furniture has often had to follow the arrival of each new information processing system.

The user can now make a choice of partial (approximately 25 line) page or full page screens, white characters on black background, black on white, green on black, or yellow on gray in color, to name a few.

KEYBOARDS

Keyboards have as many versions as there are vendors; little or no standardization has occurred. The sizes represented range from 21 x 8½ x 4 inches to 20 x 7 x 1.5 inches, flat or elevated, attached or non-attached, and bright blue to sand colors. Function keys are found on each side of the keyboard, on one side only, or across the top. However, the most important consideration for productivity and the operator's interaction with the system is that the keyboard is laid out in a logical manner. For example, if a great many functions must be accomplished using the "code" key, the code key should be located in a position of finger agility. Further, if accessing the code key requires the operator to remove his or her hand from "home" position, both time and concentration are lost.

FUNCTION KEYS

Function keys should be clearly labeled for ease of operation. Keys that effect major processing results, such as an END key and an ERASE key, should not be located together; this type of arrangement only invites disaster. However, function keys that accomplish similar tasks, such as GET and FIND, or MOVE and COPY logically belong in the same area of the keyboard. Any deviation from the standard ANSI keyboard, such as moving the shift key to another location, should not be considered in an office seeking productivity. Those offices requiring special keyboards, such as legal or accounting, should investigate whether a given system supports anything other than the standard.

PRINTER CAPABILITIES

Most manufacturers have made a conscious decision to support one of two types of printers: Diablo or Qume. Though there are exceptions, the Diablo printer is most likely to be utilized for proportional spacing and the Qume printer for standard 10, 12, or 15 characters per inch. The IBM-manufactured Qume-type printer supports proportional as well as standard typestyles. The most important point here is that a thorough investigation of software and hardware printing specifications should be conducted prior to making printer acquisition decisions.

Multi-On-Line Fonts or Dual-Head Printers

Several systems offer dual-head printers to allow for printing to take place from two printwheels at a time. This feature enables special Greek or engineering symbols to be accessed without printer interruption. This type of printer is offered by both Qume and Diablo.

Printer Sharing

As stated earlier, printer sharing is complementary to the standalone environment as a method to reduce the overall cost of hardware. Most printers can support up to three or four terminals. As documents become ready for printing by each operator, they are placed in a print queue that carries out the printing function automatically. As the printer sits idle a great deal of the time when devoted to a single station, this feature makes better use of the printer. Efficient software will support an override of the printing queue function to allow for emergency situations.

AUTOMATIC PAPER AND ENVELOPE FEEDERS

Microprocessor-oriented word processor vendors rapidly adopted single sheet as well as continuous form paper feeders, as shown in Figure 2–6 (the AB Dick Magna III and sheet feeder); however, technology has lagged behind for many in providing automatic envelope feed. Envelope feed is so necessary to productivity that it became a de facto standard prior to its arrival. Combined with printer sharing capability, these devices allow greater use of the printer during lunch hours, as well as after office hours.

DISK DRIVES

Standards for disk drives are set by the industry manufacturers. Disk drives are offered in single or double configurations and manufactured in three diameter sizes: 3.5-inch (mini), 5.25-inch, and 8-inch; each system provides only one size option. The decision to purchase a unit with a single disk drive is usually made for economic reasons. Because of the increased

Figure 2-6 AB Dick Magna III With Sheet Feeder. (*Courtesy AB Dick Corporation.*)

size of word processing operating systems and the need to keep programs resident in memory, dual disk drive systems have become a hardware standard for productivity. The acquisition of a dual disk drive with double density has proven to be the most productive path to follow. The smaller disk drives and their smaller capacity diskettes have limitations in number of pages they can store. Some such systems offer a "hard disk" facility. These disks are permanently coupled with the processor. A hard disk will generally hold 10 million or more characters, with the only drawback being lack of portability.

PHYSICAL CONSIDERATIONS

Considerable discussion involving the use of CRTs (Cathode Ray Tubes), or VDTs (Visual Display Terminals) has taken place, both in the office and in the halls of Congress. Unions representing VDT operators have claimed that office workers are suffering from psychological and physical effects such as back, neck, and arm aches, eye strain, cataracts, and nervous tension. Further claims suggest that the radiation from these terminals have caused women to suffer miscarriages and their offspring to suffer birth defects.

The Service Employees International Union (SEIU) and 9 to 5, the National Association of Working Woman, will press for state regulations and legislation to secure radiation and ergonometric protection. The SEIU has pursued the route of state legislation "because federal legislation is seen as too lengthy a process." In Chapter 4 of this book, the physical considerations of working at a VDT are discussed.[1]

In a preliminary statement in May of 1984, the National Institute for Occupational Safety and Health (NIOSH)[2] suggested that any negative evidence due to VDT or CRT exposure was "relatively minor." Though NIOSH agreed that their evidence was "incomplete," their preliminary report suggested they were in a position to answer some "fundamental questions" about the safety of VDT-type systems:

- VDTs were not found to be a source of dangerous radiation.
- There is some evidence that VDTs can increase both physical and emotional stress.
- They could not rule out VDTs as a physiologic mechanism which could impair the reproductive function, but preliminary findings did not show this to be a factor. However, a major epidemiologic study on the subject is planned by the organization.

Several considerations require attention when VDTs are being used in an office environment. Glare control is a factor in diminishing fatigue. Persons using CRTs actually require less

---

[1]Dan Trigoboff, "Unions Urge VDT Safety Laws," *MIS Week*, 19 December, 1984, p. 4.

[2]Lloyd Schwartz, "Agency: Little Ground for VDT Health Perils," *MIS Week*, 23 May, 1984, p. 22.

light than normal, but glare control is mandatory. An operator should not face a window nor have the glare of sunlight on the CRT. Attention to chair adjustability is important as is the distance of the screen from the operator. No one should sit for long periods of time staring at a CRT without periodic rest breaks. Periodic vision tests are recommended; however, there is little evidence that CRT use is more detrimental to permanent vision than any other type of close work.

DISCUSSION QUESTIONS

1. Define the term "de facto standard."
2. List three ways that word processing systems allow for insertion of new text.
3. Why is full cursor movement important in the text editing mode?
4. How does the "glossary" function help in text editing?
5. Explain the purpose of the GET, COPY, and GO TO function keys.
6. Why is format control important?
7. Explain the meaning of "intelligent work station." Give three examples of these systems.
8. What is unique about fourth generation word processors?
9. Where should function keys be located on a keyboard?
10. How does the presence of dual disk drives improve productivity?

3

Applying De Facto Standards and Concepts to Applications

Many word processing operators will recall that their minds went blank the first time they received a request to keyboard a document immediately following the completion of their hands-on training. All the hands-on training they had been through somehow did not relate to what they were asked to do. For newly trained word processing personnel, this type of experience is normal, as they have been accustomed to a tutorial environment. Though going "blank" can be tolerated for a certain period of time, a professional word processor must be able to perceive quickly how to proceed with a given task.

The word processing professional should understand the equipment's capabilities and functions; the keyboarding procedures; the revision, storage, and recall concepts of the software; and the paper path of documents within the company or organization. Given these tools, the professional can confidently approach and successfully apply the de facto standards of an information processor.

To understand how the de facto standards are applied, the document's requirements should be thoroughly examined and analyzed prior to keyboarding. This process is called the Task Analysis Procedure.

TASK ANALYSIS PROCEDURES

When you learned how to touch type and create documents on the typewriter as a student, you were first told where to set the margins, how many lines to place on a page, and probably whether to type the document in 10 or 12 characters per inch. Although those adjustments were made directly on the typewriter, the requirements were standards for the document.

In a word processing environment, requirements will probably be set by the person originating or creating the information within the document according to his or her preference.

These preferences or requirements are now performed by the format de facto standards of the particular hardware. Though simple format instructions, these standards are an example of the pre-keyboarding decisions that must be made; however, there are a great many other decisions made before and during the production of a document.

The process for making these decisions is called the Task Analysis Procedure. It should be kept in mind that the more complicated the document, the more important it is to complete each step, and to put the analysis into a written format. The steps of this analysis are described below.

Complexity Analysis

Carefully look over the document to be keyboarded. Is the subject matter complicated or difficult to understand? Are there any unusual format changes? Are special characters required that are not represented on the equipment? Are there frequently repeated phrases, sentences, paragraphs or headings?

Repetitive Analysis

If any of the material has been previously typed, was it recorded on magnetic media within the organization? Will this material be used again by this individual or others, and in what form?

Production Analysis

What functions should be incorporated to make the document easier to keyboard and retrieve? What procedures should be followed to assure a professional document, both in organization and appearance?

In summary, how can the concepts and de facto standards of word processing be applied in the most effective manner to keyboard and produce the document? Once these questions have been researched and addressed, the functions and features that can be used to produce the document in the most efficient manner must be decided upon.

USING FUNCTIONS: AN EXAMPLE

After analyzing the task to be accomplished, the de facto standards resident in the particular information processor being used are mentally reviewed and applied, reflecting the answers to the questions in the task analysis procedures. This is the time when the proper function decisions are made. As we have learned from analyzing the de facto standards, there are a number of approaches to accomplishing a word processing task. To illustrate such an approach, the following example addresses a typical decision necessary in making a format change.

A typical menu screen to perform a FORMAT change will look like the one found in Figure 3–1. As you can see, most of the initial format decisions for a document would be made from this screen.

An operator was given a 15-page, double-spaced document to be keyboarded. However, the first few pages involving the introduction had to be keyboarded in single spacing. The first impulse is to set up the document for single spacing and later use the "Change Line Spacing" format function to change to double spacing. Step 1 in the Task Analysis Procedure sug-

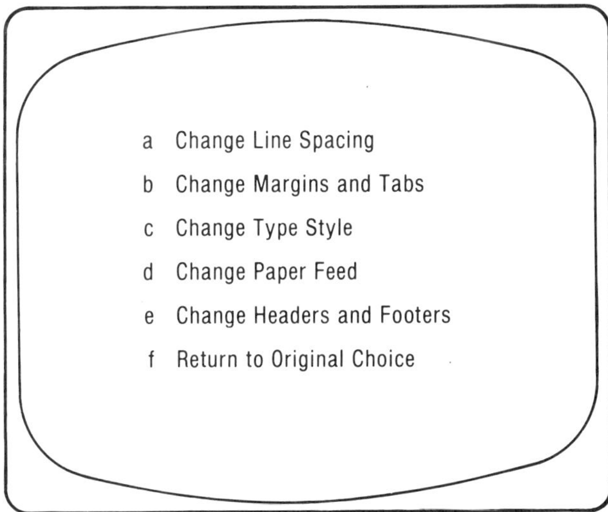

Figure 3-1   Typical format menu screen introduction.

gests that the document be visually scanned to determine if any unusual format changes exist. Because we have examined the entire document first, we know that the main requirement is for double spacing. Though the decision here is basically simple—that of format—it can have a major impact on the production of the document. In this case, the original format should be set for double spacing with the format change for single spacing appearing on the first page. A return to format is then placed at the point where the double spacing begins, as seen in Figure 3–2.

A basic productivity rule of keyboarding requires that the predominant format of a document be established in the origi-

---

INTRODUCTION

F   The following document illustrates the proper usage of format changes. You will note that this document is utilizing single spacing in the introduction, and then changes to double spacing for the rest of the document.

BODY OF DOCUMENT

RF   At this point the return to format instruction has been given and the bulk of the text requirement of double spacing is carried out. The primary rule here is that the predominant format of a document be established in the original setup, with exceptions provided for in the format change option.

F = Format change to single spacing

RF = Return to original format

Figure 3-2   Format Changes.

nal setup, with exceptions provided for in the format change option.

DOCUMENTING PROCEDURES

Nothing frustrates or inhibits productivity more in a word processing environment than when an operator or supervisor has failed to document the procedures used in creating a document. A full documentation of procedures should always be completed for a project, whether large or small. The reality of the office environment will find personnel absent due to illness and vacations, or sometimes leaving without prior notice. The lack of documentation wastes time and necessitates additional decision making.

Upon completion of the Task Analysis Procedure, the documentation of a project includes the following:

1. Name given for the document on the media.
2. Date the document was created and the originating person or department.
3. Format instructions, such as spacing, margins, typestyle, etc.
4. Location and name of the disk storage, whether external or internal disk.
5. Any special information such as incorporation of standard paragraphs, stored formats, paper drawers for the printer, etc.

A sample form for documentation of procedures is found in Figure 3–3.

In review, there are three stages, other than the keyboarding, to be followed for every project:

- Follow the four steps in the Task Analysis Procedure.
- Analyze the concepts involved in the document and select the best de facto standard to accomplish the task.
- Fully document all procedures.

SAMPLE DOCUMENTATION FORM

Name of Document:	Date Document Created: MO/DA/YR
Type of Document:	Originating Dept.:

Spacing:	Typestyle:
Margins:	
Disk Name:	Disk Document Name:
Special Requirements:	

Name of Keyboarding Person:

DOCUMENTATION NOTES:

Figure 3-3   Sample form for documentation of procedures.

APPLYING CONCEPTS TO APPLICATIONS

As can be seen from the list of de facto standards, there are several choices within functions that ultimately achieve the same end. We have learned that choosing the correct function is the key to productive word processing. In the following section, we will look at several sample documents and complete the steps in a Task Analysis, consider the functions to be used for the document's production, and document all procedures. In these examples, functions are compared relative to the task to be accomplished, and the reasons for their final adoption are shown. Though the names of the functions may vary from system to system, they are fully described in the de facto standards section of Chapter 2, and may be referred to if there is any confusion as to the particular feature chosen or its performance.

The applications and suggested procedures assume that a fourth generation word processor is available for the production of the sample exercises incorporated in this text. In some instances, more than one de facto standard will be considered as a method to accomplish the particular keyboarding task.

APPLICATION EXERCISES

Application 1

Description. The first sample document discussed is a mixture of 60 handwritten and typed pages. The subject matter deals with engineering and construction specifications, and there are numerous repetitive paragraphs.

The text is to be double spaced with some indented, single-spaced paragraphs, righthand justified and printed in Letter Gothic at 12 pitch (12 characters per inch). Portions of the document will be used again to create new specifications.

TASK ANALYSIS PROCEDURE

After reviewing the document, it has been determined that its requirements are fairly straightforward, though it does incor-

Setup: A common term in word processing to describe format of a document.

porate a number of indented paragraphs when the engineering specifications occur. It appears that a great deal of time can be saved by keyboarding and storing the repetitive engineering specification paragraphs.

Since the document is partially typed, an investigation should be made to determine the location of the disk so that the format of the original document can be reviewed and analyzed for setup. Further examination should include:

Hard Copy: A print-out on paper of the contents of a computer medium.

- Is the material in a format to be easily extracted, i.e., was the setup established according to the company's standards? Are the paragraphs to be copied scattered throughout the document?
- Is a hard copy available to determine the system page numbers so that the needed material can be found easily?
- If not magnetically stored, are there enough typewritten pages of sufficient quality to utilize OCR (Optical Character Reading) input?

FUNCTION USE

Keyboarding

After reviewing the document, it was determined that the document media could not be retrieved, due to the prior operator's failure to document the earlier project.

The reviewer determined that the copy quality was too poor to be read by the OCR scanner. The decision was made to rekeyboard the entire project.

Format

Originally, the document was double spaced. Since the indented, single-spaced format change is consistently the same, the change format function will be used for the indented paragraphs. These format change steps should be stored in a phrase library or glossary, whichever feature is present, and recalled when needed, thus saving considerable time as it will not be necessary to recreate the format change each time it appears.

Paragraph Assembly

The standard engineering specification paragraphs are stored by using a phrasing, glossary, or library function; library and the GET or COPY function can be used to retrieve the paragraphs in the order required.

Standard Document Disks

The originator has determined that certain paragraphs will be used in future documents, so a standard document diskette will be created. Those paragraphs can then be copied from disk to disk when required. A copy of the standard paragraphs should be given to all operators involved with this type of document.

The same rules apply when using shared-logic systems. In this project, the standard paragraphs are stored internally on the CPU's hard disk, and each operator is supplied with a manual of material stored on the system.

Summary of Concepts

Whenever possible, documents should be standardized to achieve productive results. Most word processors incorporate a default format which includes margins, size of paper, number of lines per page, size of line, etc., and which should be utilized as the basic standard format within an organization whenever possible. If these defaults do not meet the majority of projects produced, the software can be permanently altered to better reflect the way a company functions. However, the format change function should be used only when exceptions are required.

In this sample document, the concept was to use a phrasing function to insert the common format change rather than a copy function, where the operator would have to scroll back through the pages to copy and then move the format change. Obviously, the former method is quicker and more productive.

Because the standard paragraphs were to be used over and over, the concept of paragraph assembly is sugggested rather than phrasing or glossary. Since the repetitive paragraphs have a shared requirement, they should be recorded on a common "standard documents" disk, or on a hard disk in a shared environment.

SAMPLE DOCUMENT NO.1

Name of Document: No.1	**Date Document Created:** 9/15/YR
Type of Document: Engineering Specifications	**Originating Dept.:** Projects

Spacing: Double* **Margins:** Standard	**Typestyle:** Letter Gothic, 12 pitch
Disk Name: Spec1	**Disk Document Name:** Eng. Proj.50

Special Requirements: Standard paragraphs were created from Engineering Standards, Disk No.6.

Name of Keyboarding Person: Bill Pearson

DOCUMENTATION NOTES: *Standard for the document; single spacing in stored format called "FC1"

Figure 3-4 Documentation of procedures.

Documentation of the pre-keyboarding decisions of Application 1 can be found in Figure 3–4.

Application 2

Description. This project is composed of 10 pages of handwritten statistical documents, covering the company's financial position for the past three-year period.

Each page includes common descriptive lines and column headings. The multi-columns are to be typed in single spacing. There is a strong probability that the columns will be moved during the editing process.

The format of the document will be used again each year.

TASK ANALYSIS PROCEDURE

As there are approximately 13 columns plus a descriptive column, the 15-pitch print capability will probably be necessary to fit the project on the page.

The many similar headings and formats can be used from page to page of the document. The headings and columnar format should be saved for future use.

A variety of tabs will be used in this document, such as left flush tabs for descriptions, center tabs for headings, decimal tabs for automatic alignment of the numbers, and righthand flush tabs for column descriptions. The math function, if present, can be used for proofing.

FUNCTION USE

Column Layout (Setup)

Using the automatic column layout function, it is possible to set up the document very quickly; the system does all the spacing calculations and aligns the column with proper outside and inside margins. This function is important to a financial document, as it provides the ability to move columns during the revision phase of the document.

Phrasing or Glossary

The vertical text describing line items can be keyboarded by using phrasing or glossary for storing. In financial documents, headings of the past, present, and forecast years will usually stay the same. By phrasing the line descriptions and the column headings, each new page can be established simply by recalling these two pre-stored documents.

Math Functions

Once financial documents have been keyboarded, the math functions can assist in the proofing of tables and totals.

Keystroke Save

If the software supports the "keystroke save" or a "stored keystroke" function, the math functions used to perform the proofing operation can be stored with the page, thus saving time in the machine proofing phase.

Multiple Print Standards

The number of columns on the page requires that the document be printed in 15 pitch (15 characters to the inch). This type of flexibility often enables large documents to be typed on standard paper.

Summary of Concepts

The choice of column layout in this project accomplishes two goals of word processing: increased productivity and professional appearance. Individual tab stops could be set and finite adjustments made to set up columns manually; however, considerable additional time would have been consumed by such a procedure. By incorporating a phrasing feature, many keystrokes are saved in producing this complicated document.

Documentation of Application 2 can be found in Figure 3–5.

Application 3

Description. The project is a list of 500 employees and includes the following personnel data concerning their employment:

- Complete Name of Employee
- Home Address

SAMPLE DOCUMENT NO.2

Name of Document: No.2	**Date Document Created:** 11/15/YR
Type of Document: Financial	**Originating Dept.:** Accounting

Spacing: Single	**Typestyle:** Letter Gothic 15′
Margins: Left: 10 Right: 155	
Disk Name: ACCT2	**Disk Document Name:** Fin 84

Disk Storage Location: Central Files

Special Requirements: Place 8½ x 11 paper horizontally in paper feed for printing.

NOTE: Do not erase!

Name of Keyboarding Person: Bill Jones

DOCUMENTATION NOTES: Column layout utilized is stored in phrasing library under "C". Vertical descriptions in phrasing library under "D."

Figure 3-5   Documentation of procedure.

- Home Phone
- Date of Hire
- Position within Company
- Employed Department
- Business Extension
- Current Salary
- Group Insurance Coverage*
  Level and Description of Coverage
- Date of Last Physical
- Training Classes Required and
  Up-to-Date List of Classes Completed*

TASK ANALYSIS PROCEDURE

Shell Document: A document format prepared for merging and printing text or file information previously recorded.

The application requires various functions of records processing, such as creating file descriptions, list processing, and merging. Because many people will use the information, the file design should be presented to the originator prior to the actual creation on disk. The originator should also have input regarding the final appearance parameters of the document. The operator will use these parameters to create a shell document. Standard paragraphs describing insurance coverage and education courses will be incorporated to provide the necessary merge information in fields designated for group insurance and training.

FUNCTION USE

Fields: A single unit of information within a record. A file.

The file design function is used to create the necessary fields of information. This particular file will incorporate three types of fields:

- Text—allows sentences to be created into the file
- Character—usually one or two words per field
- Math—numeric data, which may be used for comparison of dates and determining the total number of years employed, total insurance coverage, etc.

*These fields of information will have standard description prestored for inclusion where appropriate.

Include

This particular file will use the *include* function to insert variable paragraph information concerning group life insurance and training for each employee into final printed reports.

Library

A variety of paragraphs have been created that will describe the individual employee's benefits for group insurance, and de-

<table>
<tr><td colspan="4" align="center">SAMPLE DOCUMENT NO.3—FILE DESIGN</td></tr>
<tr><th>Field Name</th><th>Field Type</th><th>Number of Characters</th><th>Comments</th></tr>
<tr><td>Title</td><td>char</td><td>4</td><td></td></tr>
<tr><td>First Name</td><td>char</td><td>10</td><td></td></tr>
<tr><td>MI</td><td>char</td><td>2</td><td></td></tr>
<tr><td>Last Name</td><td>char</td><td>15</td><td></td></tr>
<tr><td>Sub Title</td><td>char</td><td>4</td><td></td></tr>
<tr><td>Home Address</td><td>char</td><td>25</td><td></td></tr>
<tr><td>City</td><td>char</td><td>15</td><td></td></tr>
<tr><td>Home Phone</td><td>char</td><td>8</td><td></td></tr>
<tr><td>Date of Hire</td><td>math</td><td>8</td><td>yr/month/day</td></tr>
<tr><td>Position</td><td>char</td><td>40</td><td></td></tr>
<tr><td>Department</td><td>char</td><td>25</td><td></td></tr>
<tr><td>Business Extension</td><td>char</td><td>4</td><td></td></tr>
<tr><td>Current Salary</td><td>math</td><td>7</td><td></td></tr>
<tr><td>Group Insurance</td><td>math</td><td>10</td><td></td></tr>
<tr><td>Group Ins. Descr.</td><td>text</td><td>200</td><td>Use include function</td></tr>
<tr><td>Date of Last Physical</td><td>math</td><td>8</td><td>yr/month/day</td></tr>
<tr><td>Training Received</td><td>text</td><td>500</td><td>Use include function</td></tr>
<tr><td>Training Required</td><td>text</td><td>300</td><td>Use include function</td></tr>
<tr><td colspan="4">Note: Libraries for include functions are under document "LIBRARY".</td></tr>
</table>

Figure 3-6   File Design Documentation.

SAMPLE DOCUMENT NO.3

Name of Document: No.3	**Date Document Created:** 10/1/YR
Type of Document: Employee File	**Originating Dept.:** Personnel

Spacing: Single	**Typestyle:** Prestige Elite
Margins:	
Disk Name: EMPL	**Disk File Name:** Empl List
Special Requirements: Note: Margins are determined by the particular merge document being utilized with this file.	**Merge Document Name(s):** Employee Insurance Employee Training Employee Status

Name of Keyboarding Person: Sally Kims

DOCUMENTATION NOTES: Library of paragraphs utilized in file design.

Figure 3-7 Documentation of procedure.

tails of his or her training plan. When a report is generated of employee status, the include statement in the insurance and training fields selects the appropriate paragraphs for each employee.

File Design

Careful pre-planning during the file design stages facilitates future utilization of a file. Those fields that require frequent updating should be designed to appear at the beginning of the file, thus allowing for more efficient data entry. Of prime importance is the necessity for using each individual field. These decisions are made within the parameters of the software capability of the system. Beta testing a file with just a few entries can save many processing problems in the future. Note that the completed file design shown in Figure 3–6 has not been put in priority order; it merely reflects the order of the originator's requirements.

Summary of Concepts

Data Base: A single file of information providing the user with a wide variety of related information.

Dedicated Word Processor: Used here to describe a fourth generation word processor that incorporates a microprocessor and a word processing keyboard with function keys.

The records processing feature can provide the user with numerous administrative tools. The ability to select a limited number of fields of information from a large file or data base gives the ability to create numerous reports and projects. Documentation for Application 3 can be found in Figure 3–7.

In the three applications described, the most efficient de facto standards of a dedicated word processor were incorporated. Chapter 5 will discuss how these standards are applied when using microcomputer software for word processing.

DISCUSSION QUESTIONS

1. What action should the word processing operator or supervisor take prior to the keyboarding of a document?

2. Describe the three steps of the Task Anaysis Procedure.

3. Describe how Document 1 could be produced with a single disk drive.

4. What is the most important de facto standard utilized in Document 2?

5. If you are currently training on a word/information processor, list and define the types of fields in the records processing function.

6. Properly arrange the fields in Figure 3–6 to reflect their probable usage in keeping the employee's file current.

7. What additional information would you add to the Documentation of Procedures form for each of the three sample applications?

4

Office Procedures and Practices

Though office automation has not yet achieved the goal of the "paperless office" concept envisioned by productivity consultants, the use of magnetic media for the storage of information has given us the ability to create and store drafts of documents on diskettes instead of filing them away in traditional office filing cabinets. Since diskettes are the most common magnetic media used in dedicated word processors and small business computers, a discussion of their proper usage is in order. This chapter will look at the diskette's development, physical makeup, and proper care and handling.

The latter part of the chapter discusses storage and retrieval concepts, the naming of documents, and the organization of information on the diskette.

MAGNETIC MEDIA FOR INFORMATION PROCESSING[1]

Origin of the Flexible Diskette

When IBM was searching for a functional alternative to the digital cassette as an input device for its various computer systems, it is unlikely that they could have foreseen the impact that the introduction of the flexible disk was to have on the future of the mini-micro computer field, as well as the word processing area. For the first time, the computer industry had a low-cost memory device with a faster transfer rate for recorded data, and the ability to access this data randomly. Figure 4–1 depicts the manufacturing cycle of a flexible disk.

---

[1]The majority of the information found in this section of Chapter 4 was provided by Syncom, manufacturer of flexible disks, of Mitchell, South Dakota.

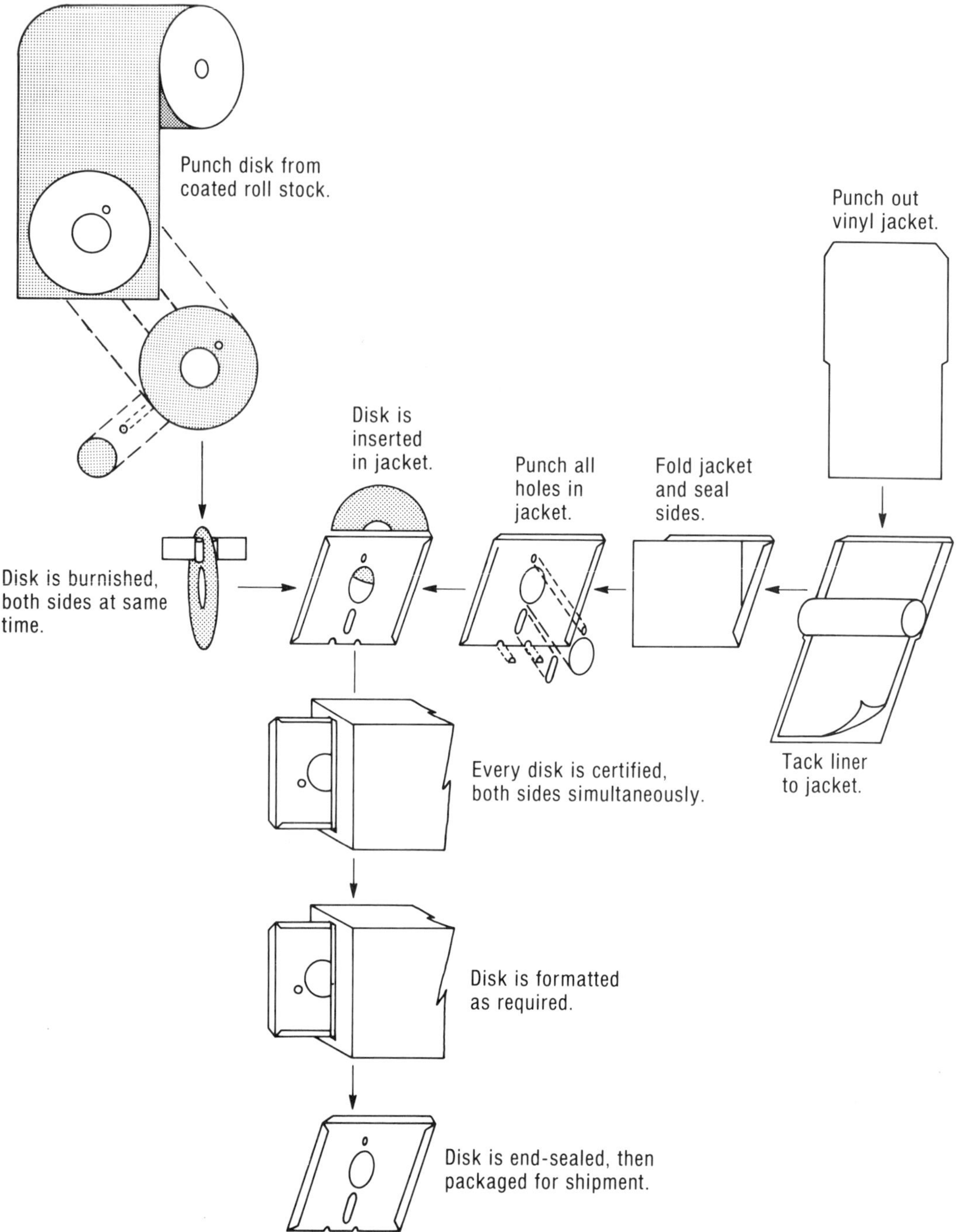

Figure 4-1 The making of a flexible disk. (*Courtesy of Syncom®, Mitchell, South Dakota.*)

There were many developments in flexible disk drives by IBM and other companies, most notably Shugart and Memorex. These three companies set the basic standards: IBM with the soft sector flexible disk drives; and Shugart and Memorex with the hard sector disk drives. In the hard sector flexible disk field, the Shugart design is given the most attention and reflects the greatest demand. It is important to remember that, even though Shugart and Memorex pioneered the hard sector flexible disk, they both manufacture drives which are compatible to the IBM flexible disk drives. The IBM flexible disk is recognized as the industry-compatible flexible disk since IBM dominates the computer field in flexible disk drive design technology. This does not mean that IBM is the largest maker of flexible disks, rather that they lead when it comes to drive advances. The Shugart and Memorex hard sector diskettes are shown in Figures 4–2 and 4–3, respectively.

The first flexible disks that appeared on the market, which are still used in a great numbers today, were the eight-inch (8″ square) flexible disks. The first developments were of what is referred to in the industry as "single density" flexible disks. This has since been followed by the development of the dual (double) and quad densities.

Initializing Diskettes

The eight-inch flexible disk was followed by the development of the 5¼-inch, or mini, flexible disk. Here, too, the development of this disk reflects the hard and soft sector technology, as well as the single and double density capabilities of the eight-inch disks.

The ability of a flexible disk to operate, or accept data, depends upon the ability to locate the data on the recording surface as the flexible disk rotates. This ability to write or read data on a flexible disk depends on the initializing (or formatting) of the flexible disk. This process can be compared to a road map, or directory, of the disk's surface so that the reading or writing function of the drive knows where to put, or retrieve, information on the flexible disk surface. When using a soft sector flexible disk, the flexible disk must be initialized before being shipped to the customer or the customer must have the ability to initialize (format) on the machine he or she uses prior to recording data on the disk.

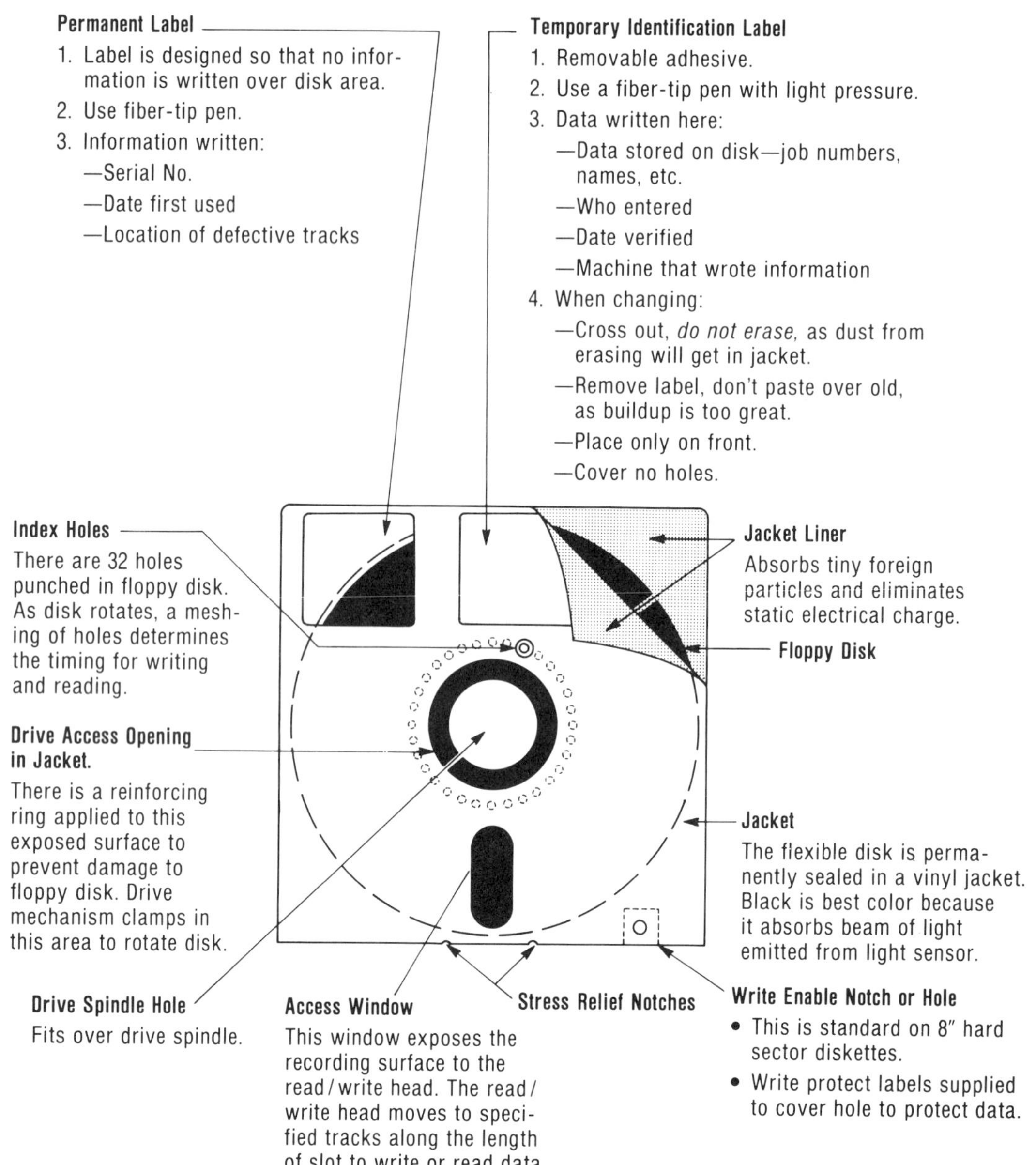

Figure 4-2 Shugart-compatible hard sector diskette. (*Courtesy of Syncom®, Mitchell, South Dakota.*)

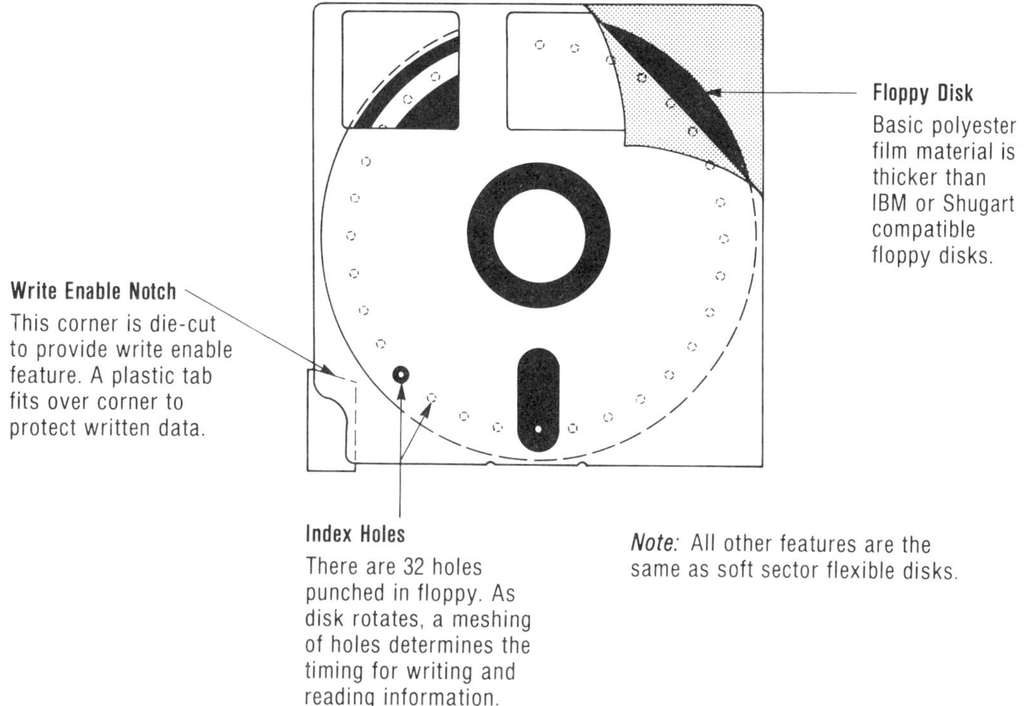

Figure 4-3   Memorex-compatible hard sector diskette. (*Courtesy of Syncom®, Mitchell, South Dakota.*)

When using a hard sector flexible disk, initializing does not have to be done by the manufacturer. The location of the holes in a circle will, by mechanical means, automatically guide, or direct, the reading/writing function of the flexible disk drive by breaking the flexible disk surface into sectors.

The emphasis here is on the need to initialize (electronically sector) before shipment or to sector by means of a series of holes in the flexible disk surface. The disk formats can be seen in Figure 4–4.

SOFT SECTOR

A flexible disk is soft sectored when it has only one index hole, as shown in Figure 4–4. Each track is divided into sectors by electronic timing after sensing the index hole on each revolution. The number of sectors depends upon format required for

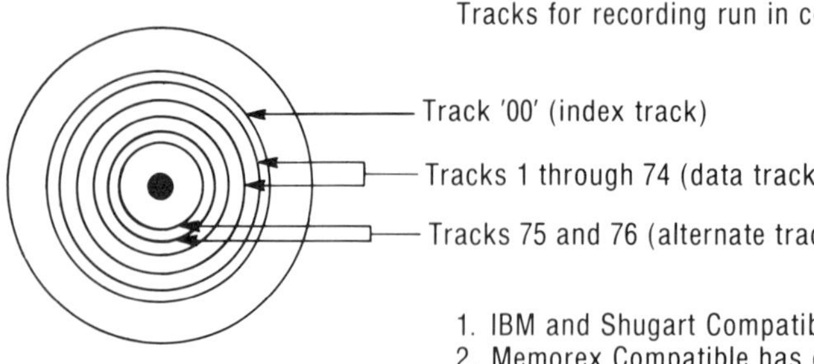

1. IBM and Shugart Compatible have 77 tracks.
2. Memorex Compatible has only 64 tracks.
3. The difference between single and double density is packing more bits per inch on a track, not increasing the number of tracks.

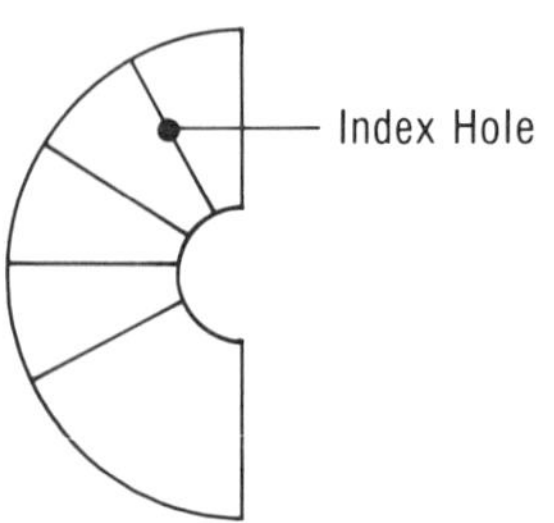

Soft Sector

A flexible disk is soft sectored when it has only one index hole. Each track is divided into sectors by electronic timing after sensing the index hole on each revolution. The number of sectors depend upon format required for each soft sectored flexible disk. Syncom's Flexible Diskette Format Specification Sheet No. S-10220 indicates the number of sectors required for each soft sector available. All IBM drives or IBM compatible flexible disk drives use soft sector diskettes.

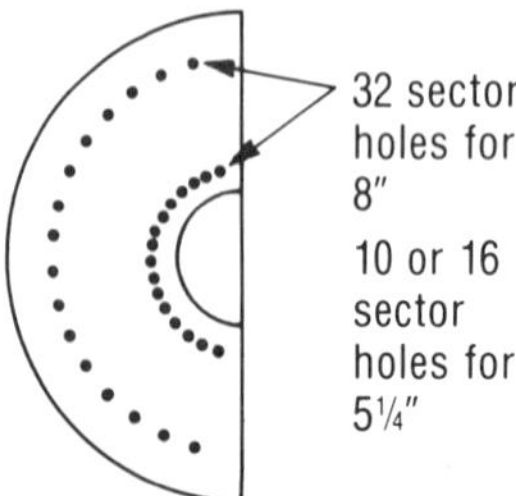

Hard Sector

A flexible disk that is hard sectored has the index holes punched right into the disk. The number of holes depends on the size of the flexible disk. These holes divide up each track into sectors by a light beam physically sensing each hole. Syncom's Flexible Diskette Format Specification Sheet No. S-10220 indicates the different types of hard sector diskettes offered.

Figure 4-4　Flexible disk tracks and sectors. (*Courtesy of Syncom®, Mitchell, South Dakota.*)

each soft-sectored flexible disk. All IBM drives or IBM-compatible flexible disk drives use soft sector diskettes.

HARD SECTOR

A flexible disk that is hard sectored has the index holes punched right into the disk (see Figure 4–4). The number of holes depends on the size of the flexible disk. These holes divide each track into sectors by having a light beam physically sense each hole.

Special Formats

Some manufacturers of microcomputers or dedicated word processors have developed their own (or special) formatted flexible disks that will work only in their equipment. Disk suppliers have decoded some of these special formats; however, the equipment manufacturers have initiated court suits against these disk suppliers and they will not approve the use of third party disks.

Care and Handling of Flexible Disks

Though the flexible disk is encased in a sturdy envelope, it should be treated with utmost care as many common office items and occurrences can cause damage to flexible disks and the ultimate loss of information.

MAGNETS

Enemy number one of the magnetic disk, or any other magnetic media, is the magnet. Though magnets are not commonly found in the office, the bell-ringing telephone is a common magnet-bearing device. Other culprits are the magnets found on copy holders, and paper clips stored in magnetic holders. Any metallic device has the potential for holding a magnetic charge, and care should be given to avoid placing such objects on or near diskettes.

HEAT

Diskettes should never be left in direct sunlight or in places where temperatures are excessive, such as in closed automobiles or in their trunks.

LIQUIDS

It is particularly important not to use a disk if its surface has been contaminated with sticky fluids (soft drinks, coffee) or abrasive substances, such as metal filings. Placing a contaminated diskette in a disk drive can contaminate the read/write head, causing operating errors. In addition, contaminants can be passed to clean disks. A substance spilled on the disk jacket can sometimes be removed; the data can usually be recovered only if the contaminant does not reach the recording surface. After recovering the data, the disk should be copied and the old one discarded.

OTHER DANGERS

The smallest scratch from a staple or a fingernail can cause a read/write head to jump over the contamination. Remember, the name "flexible" disk is descriptive in nature, *not* suggestive. This product is not designed to be folded or unnecessarily flexed. Tight rubber bands that cause the disk to bend should be avoided. If a diskette is stored for a lengthy period with a slight bend it will sometimes permanently assume the bend and fail to operate properly. *Never* attach paper clips to magnetic disks. Always use a felt-tipped pen when writing on disk labels; sharp-pointed pens will damage the disk's surface.

STATIC ELECTRICITY

Disks can become slightly charged with static electricity and attract contaminants that build up in the work areas, such as cigarette ashes, dust, or loose debris. When disks are not in use they should be kept in the protective tyvec envelopes provided by the manufacturer to protect the read/write slot. If static electricity is a problem around a work area, there are several methods to reduce its presence, such as anti-static mats for the floor or anti-static sprays for the carpet. The standard clear plastic carpet protectors should not be used around CRTs if static electricity is a problem.

HANDLING DISKETTES

Although the diskette is housed in a protective vinyl jacket, which it never leaves, the following tips will offer maximum life and reliability.

1. To remove a disk from its envelope, grasp the disk by its upper edge and pull, as in Figure 4–5.
2. When inserting the disk into the drive opening, be gentle. Don't force it in if resistance is encountered. If

If stored outside the stated limits, flexible disks should be conditioned in the operating environment to ensure proper performance. Conditioning time for flexible disks is at least five minutes.

Data Recovery

If disk errors occur, decisions must be made regarding the replacement of the individual disk. The following guidelines apply mainly to microcomputer users:

1. When using a new disk, assign a serial number to it and record that number on the disk's permanent label. An example of a serial number would be the year, month and day, such as 85–3–22. Keep a log of disk serial numbers to estimate the wear of a particular disk. (See sections *Naming Diskettes* and *Naming Projects* later in this chapter.)

2. Whenever a disk error occurs on the same track repeatedly, re-initialize the disk as soon as possible. Periodic examination of the disk serial numbers will help determine if the disk is too old to continue using. If there are more than two defective tracks, the disk should be replaced.

3. *Disk Irregularities.* Although flexible disks rarely develop irregularities through wear, irregularities may occur if some foreign material has gotten on the diskette. If an error occurs on a flexible disk (the particular system will alert the operator should this happen), the operator should take several steps:

- *Copy the data.* Each installation should have a standard procedure to be followed in case a data record cannot be read or written onto a diskette. If the station has the copy function, the best data recovery procedure is to copy the data onto a new diskette and manually key in the missing records or text.

- *Re-initialize the disk.* The operator should make note of diskette irregularities on the external label of the diskette. After data on an irregular track has been recovered and copied to a new disk, the problem disk should be re-initialized.

- As part of the initialization routine, the device assigns track and sector numbers to the disk, bypasses the defective track, and assigns the track number of the defective track to the next good track. Two defective tracks per disk can be replaced in this manner.

- Do not use a disk with a defective area before re-initializing it to bypass the track containing the defective area. Then record the number of the defective track on the permanent label.

DOCUMENT STORAGE AND RETRIEVAL CONCEPTS

In Chapter 3, we learned the importance of documenting the set-up procedures of a project to assist in its re-use or revision. Naming disks and documents in a logical and meaningful manner is important to the retrieval of information stored on magnetic media.

In some cases, the software will dictate how diskettes and documents can be named by limiting the number of letters, or by restricting the type of keyboard characters that may be used. Whatever the case, a naming system should be designed and followed strictly.

Naming Diskettes

As we have discussed earlier in this chapter, each diskette should be given a serial number to track usage and frequency of disk errors. These numbers are for internal tracking only and should not be used as a disk naming method. Most systems will require that work diskettes be named, a process that must be carried out prior to using a new disk.

As a student, you may have named your training disk "MARY" or "JOHN." However, in a business environment, disks should reflect an organization's structure and size. For example, there is little necessity to name disks by departments when an organization has only a few employees or functions. However, if the operation of a company involves manufacturing, sales, public relations, and accounting functions, a procedure to name disks by departments would be in order. Most systems allow for six letters or numbers, or a combination thereof. Some examples of naming disks are shown below:

S1	Sales Department
ACTG1	Accounting Department
PR:1	Public Relations
M1/85	Manufacturing

As a cross-reference to locate disks, the name given to a disk can be written next to the serial number in the master log of diskettes.

Naming Documents

Since far more documents or projects are named than diskettes, it is especially important that careful thought be given to their naming.

SIZE OF NAME

Since the name of the document must be rekeyed into the system whenever it is to be accessed, the name should be as short as possible. Compare the two document name choices below for a divorce settlement prepared by an attorney named Brown in March of 1985.

Choice No. 1 The First Divorce Decreee Prepared by Attorney
              Brown, 3/85
Choice No. 2 ddb:385

The obvious choice is No. 2, as it uses the standard document initials of "Divorce Decree" followed by the last initial of the attorney, "*Brown*," and also incorporates the date. The shorter the name chosen for the document, the less incidence there is for error.

If the word processing system or program allows for a comment section to decribe the document's contents, further elaboration can be placed there. Otherwise, additional description can be placed in a log or on a printed hard copy of the disk's contents.

UPPER AND LOWER CASE

A document's exact name must be entered each time it is used, and in some systems, lower and upper case is differentiated. If so, standards for upper and lower case will make recall simpler. Such a practice would suggest using all lower case letters for the names of documents, and all upper case letters for storing the names of records processing setups or standard documents. As noted below, this concept would list the new documents (lower case names) in the directory first.

Documentation on Hard Copy and Logging

Whatever the methods for storing a hard copy of a final document, the name of the disk used and the document's name should be written on the first page. Some organizations find that having a stamp for this purpose encourages accurate documentation. For example:

Disk Name: _______________________
Document Name: ______________
Originating Dept.: ______________
Date: ___________________________

Diskette Directory Organization

Most dedicated word processors provide an automatic index feature which enters the name of the document into the diskette index at the time it is created. Further, this index can be viewed by the operator when necessary. A copy of the index may be printed, and should be retained with the disk for quick identification of its contents. In non-standalones, this is achieved using directory and printing utilities.

Each system has its own sorting priority; that is, it decides the order in which the names will appear in the index. The IBM Displaywriter, for example, places all lower case names first in alphabetical order, all capitalized names next, and then

SYSTEM INDEX

Diskette Name:	*Space Available:*	*Space Unusable:*

DOCUMENT NAME:	ap
DOCUMENT TYPE:	document
COMMENT:	shell for accounts payable listing
DOCUMENT NAME:	bdd85
DOCUMENT TYPE:	document
COMMENT:	brown divorce document — 3/85
DOCUMENT NAME:	enrpt2
DOCUMENT TYPE:	file
COMMENT:	second engineering report file
DOCUMENT NAME:	APL
DOCUMENT TYPE:	setup
COMMENT:	output setup for accounts payable listing
DOCUMENT NAME:	1985
DOCUMENT TYPE:	document
COMMENT:	standards for calendar schedule

Figure 4-7   Sample system index.

all documents identified by or starting with numbers. Such an index would sequence as shown in Figure 4-7.

Document Storage

Much confusion reigns over the concept of document storage; in reality, document storage must be thought of in short-term, long-term, and permanent concepts. Depending upon the type of system(s) being used for word processing—i.e., whether floppy disk, hard disk, or a combination of both—projects should be recorded on either a "Daily" disk, a "Long-Term" disk, or a "Basic/Standard Document" disk. In the case of storage on a fixed disk, specific areas, or libraries, are designated for short- and long-term storage. Determining the time length of document storage and their retrieval methods are discussed in the following paragraphs.

DAILY WORK DISKS

Short-term, or daily projects, are retained on magnetic media only for the period of time it takes for the originator to approve, or sign, the final version—put another way, until the document is sent in the mail.

However, before the document is deleted from the disk, an analysis of the document's future use should be made. Perhaps the letter is one written to a policy holder who raised a question about a new type of insurance. If the question is considered one that would probably occur again, consideration should be given to reformatting the letter to allow for a variable merge, or, if records processing is available, for merging information from a file, and placing it in permanent storage. If no future use is seen for the letter or document, it should be erased from the daily work disk, or area of the fixed disk, when the finished product reaches the mail.

In either case, it is important that an organization have a policy about storage retention times to guard against the unintentional loss of information. Using concepts of document creation, this same type of long-term usage is perhaps more beneficial if conducted prior to the creation of any document.

LONG-TERM STORAGE

Documents should be considered for long-term storage when any of the following characteristics exist:

- It is anticipated that the project will undergo a number of revisions.
- The project has a number of authors.
- Portions of the project cannot be completed until additional information is received.
- Final format instructions are not available.
- The document's content must be reviewed and/or approved by a number of people.

As in the case of short-term documents, an analysis of the potential future use of the basic document should be made once the project is completed.

PERMANENT STORAGE

Documents that fall into the permanent storage classification are formatted in such a way that they can be adapted for multiple uses. An example of such a document would be the engineering specifications in Application 1 discussed in Chapter 3. This project consisted of standard paragraphs that are continuously selected in preparing engineering specifications. These paragraphs would be placed in permanent storage, available for all operators to use, either on floppy disks or on a fixed disk, depending upon the system being utilized.

Permanent storage should be reserved for those documents approved by management as authoritative and useful for future projects. Some provision should be made, however, to review permanent storage on a routine basis, as statistics and conditions do change with alarming frequency.

ARCHIVING

When a distributed system is being used for word/information processing and a number of terminals are involved, most organizations will require that all documents be archived to floppy disks or in some cases to magnetic tape. This practice allows for maximum memory to be available for all the system's users.

THE WORK ENVIRONMENT

Document Appeal

One of the exciting aspects of using word processing capability is the prospect of creating the perfect document. The chances of meeting this goal have continually improved over the years with the technology advances in function. The successful user of word processing will consider the following when preparing a document:

GRAMMAR, PUNCTUATION, AND SPELLING

Language arts skills should be everyone's concern, but none more so than people involved in a word processing environment. These skills must be learned; they cannot be faked. The degree to which an individual will be called upon to use these skills will depend upon the size and policies of an organization. Some authors do not appreciate having their grammar or punctuation changed; in this case, a supervisor or proofer should be notified when a grammatical or punctuation error is noted. In most cases, however, word processing operators are expected to correct any such errors.

FORMATTING A DOCUMENT

Most organizations have established standard formats for letters, legal documents, engineering specifications, etc. However, occasionally a document calls for special presentation, e.g., hanging indentions with bold-face headings. Understanding the many options available on a particular system for adding variety to a document's appearance is extremely important in word/information processing. The ability to change margins and typefaces and spacing easily, to provide indented formats, and to incorporate headers and footers provides the operator with "instant artist" tools not available to those who must produce documents on a standard typewriter.

Proofreading Techniques

A number of proofreading approaches, or methods, are prevalent in today's office. Nothing defeats professionalism more than typos and recurring errors.

Not everyone makes a good proofreader; proofreading is a skill. However, a number of techniques for proofreading one's own work, if this is required, can eliminate many of the typos and assist in elevating the professionalism of word processing.

MACHINE SPELLING CHECKS

If a spelling program exists on the software, by all means, it should be used to check the document. However, spelling programs are not infallible; they make mistakes. Further, they will not detect when a wrong or duplicate word has been typed; this determination must be made by the operator and/or proofer. As an example, see how many errors you can detect in the following paragraph: There are nine errors, yet only one involves a misspelled word that would have been detected by a spelling check program. The errors are revealed in Discussion Question 1 at the end of this chapter.

"The biggest cost justification for the system in online billing," Mr. Jones notes. "We can"t move a piece of freight without a bill, and procession the paperwork used to slow us down. Now, thanks to the system's quick response time, we can cut between 3,500 and 4000 freight bills a day. On pre-paid orders—which comprise half of out business—we can get bills out within hours. If the the frieght comes in at 5 p.m. Monday, we can have a bill and statement at the post office by 6 a.m Tuesday. This has already improved ours accounts receivable by 25 to 30 percent."

If you found them all the first time, you are well on your way to acquiring proofreading techniques. Chances are, however, that you did not find them all the first time. The nine errors represent some of the most common typographical errors and omissions. Some typical errors are:

- Reversing letters—a common error due to either weak vs. strong fingers, or caused by anticipating letters.
- Hitting keys next to the one desired.
- Leaving out letters.
- Repeating words or phrases.

Some basic techniques can be applied in proofreading typewritten material. Some experts suggest a scanning process—scanning once for appearance and format; again for typos, grammar and punctuation; and a third time for omissions, deletions, or double typed words.[2] These suggestions work well; however, some responsibility for content clarity does fall on the operator. In the above example, several mistyped words confuse the meaning of the paragraph, yet are correctly spelled words. A combination of scanning and reading for clarity will guarantee a more perfect document.

Nothing is more embarrassing than to produce 1,000 multiple, individualized letters with a typo. A time-tested technique for checking short documents, after a scanning and checking for clarity check has been completed, is to read a page *backwards*, covering the line above with a ruler. Try this technique with the indented paragraph above and notice how

---

[2] Jo Ann Rosen, "Proofreading Skills Reflect Quality Performance," *Words*, December-January 1984, p. 37–38.

quickly you can spot the errors. This would not be practical for long documents, but for one- or two-page letters it works quite well.

Working at a Video Display (VDT/CRT)

Though a great deal of discussion and research has taken place in recent months concerning VDT hazards, no definitive evidence has been found to prove that they present a health hazard to users. There are a number of user organizations who are protesting these findings, as mentioned in Chapter 2. Though the controversy continues, people who spend the major portion of their work day in front of a VDT do suffer discomfort when the following conditions are not taken into consideration.[3]

MUSCULAR DISCOMFORT

Any job or activity that requires a person to sit in one position for a long period of time will cause discomfort. This problem can be relieved by providing:

- Proper design and arrangement of the work station.
- Adjustable furniture which allows for a range of comfortable positions of both chair and display furniture.
- Periodic rest breaks.

VISUAL FATIGUE

Frequent eye examinations as prescribed by the medical profession are suggested. Visual requirements are different for VDTs than for reading hand-held printed materials, and thus may pose a problem for people who wear reading glasses or bifocals. When an eye examination is scheduled, it is suggested that the doctor be informed that the individual works with a VDT.

For those interested in further study of VDT usage, the following bibliography may be useful.

---

[3]Lloyd Schwartz, "Agency: Little Ground for VDT Health Perils," *MIS Week,* 23 May 1984, p. 22.

American Medical Association, "Effects of Physical Forces on the Reproductive Cycle," 1983.

Campbell, E.W. and K. Durden, "The VDT Issue: A Consideration of its Physiological, Psychological and Clinical Background," *Ophthal. Physics and Opt.,* Vol. 3, 1983.

DeGroot, J.P. and A. Kamphuis, "Eyestrain in VDU Users: Physical Correlates and Long-term Effects," *Human Factors Journal,* Vol. 25, 1983.

Dickerson, O.B. and W.E. Baker, "Health Considerations at the Information Work Place," VDTs: Usability Issues & Health Concerns, Stamford Conference, Prentice-Hall, 1984.

Food and Drug Administration, National Center for Devices and Radiological Health, Radiological Health Bulletin, XVII, February 2, 1983.

Greenwald, M., S. Greenwald, M. Arch and R. Blake, "Long-lasting Visual After-effect from Viewing a Computer Video Display," *New England Journal of Medicine,* Vol. 309 (5), 1983.

Rogowitz, B.E., "The Human Visual System: A Guide for the Display Technologist," *Proceedings of the SID,* Vol. 24, 1983.

Weiss, M.M., "The VDT—Is There a Radiation Hazard?" *JOM,* Vol. 25, 1983.

Care of the Equipment

The operator can be involved in minor maintenance to a computer work station by fulfilling a few housekeeping routines that, in the long run, will help productivity.

PRINTERS

Printers equipped with sheet feeders require that the platen be cleaned with a solvent to remove ink and paper dust. These two items tend to make the platen too smooth to grab the paper, thus causing paper jams. One common type of cleaner is called "Fedron," and can be acquired through an office products store.

CRTs

CRTs collect dust because of the heat and the static electricity on the surface of the screen. There are special products on the market for cleaning CRTs, such as Bates Cleaning Products for CRTs. Equipment vendors are also a source of information on this type of cleaner.

KEYBOARDS

All foreign substances, such as food, drinks, cigarette ashes, paper clips, etc. should be kept away from the electronic keyboard. Should any liquid be spilled on the keyboard, the maintenance engineer should be consulted immediately.

DISCUSSION QUESTIONS

1. Type the special paragraph to test the spell-checking program on the equipment you are currently using. The errors are:

- First sentence: "in" should be "is"
  Second sentence: "can"t" should be "can't"
  "procession" should be "processing"
  Third sentence: "4000" should be "4,000"
  Fourth sentence: "out" should be "our"
  Fifth sentence: second "the" should be eliminated
  "frieght" should be "freight"
  "a.m" should be "a.m."
  Sixth sentence: "ours" should be "our"

2. What is the difference between single and double density diskettes?
3. Is the hard sector or soft sector diskette initialized by the manufacturer?
4. What sectored disk has a single index hole?
5. Explain how a disk is initialized.
6. How can information be recovered on the equipment you are currently using?

7. Explain how this same equipment organizes document names in the diskette index.

8. When should documents be erased from storage?

9. What is the difference between "Long-Term" and "Permanent" storage?

10. How can operator fatigue be relieved?

5

Using Computers in the Word/Information Processing Environment

The world has seen a number of technology revolutions since the announcement of the UNIVAC I, the world's first computer (see Figure 5–1), and the ENIAC, the world's first electronic computer (see Figure 5–2). This original monster covered a floor space of 1,500 square feet, included 18,000 vacuum tubes, weighed 30 tons, and was touted as performing some 300 days of manual calculations in just one day.[1] The ENIAC now resides in the Smithsonian Institution. Significant advances in computers have occurred during the intervening years; however, the introduction of the microprocessor silicon "chip" by Intel of Santa Clara, California in 1971 led the way to a social and business phenomenon: the microcomputer.

THE MICROCOMPUTER AND WORD/INFORMATION PROCESSING

Arithmetic/Logic: That part of the processor containing the circuits that perform arithmetic and logic.

Control Section: That part of the processor that effects the retrieval and interpretation of instructions.

The uniqueness of the microprocessor chip lies in its architecture: the chip contains both the arithmetic/logic unit and a control section necessary for the processing function of a computer. The most impressive part of this capability, to those unacquainted with the inner workings of a computer, is how small physically this processing power is compared to the early ENIAC. The micro size of the processor chip, as can be seen in a comparison to the tip of a finger in Figure 5–3, has allowed computing power to be brought to the desk top.[2] Though it is not necessary for those who seek careers in information processing to comprehend the inner workings of a computer, it is important that the professional in the office environment have a speaking acquaintance with this computing power.

In the following sections we will look at the computer

---

[1]*History of Computer Systems,* Sperry, n.d.,n.p.

[2]Marilyn Bohl, *Information Processing,* 4th ed. (Chicago: Science Research Associates, Inc., 1984), p. 15.

Figure 5-1   The world's first computer, UNIVAC I. (*Courtesy of Sperry Corporation.*)

basics. The answers to such questions as: What are microprocessors? What are operating systems? and What is program software? will be discussed, so that we might have a better platform from which to address word processing software as applied to microcomputers.

What Is a Computer?

In describing its hardware and software components to the uninitiated, a computer or information processor might be compared with the operation of an automobile. A car has all of the innate capability of traveling far and wide, but without the additional ingredient of intelligence, it cannot travel the first inch. It is merely an orderly combination of many types of materials—just so much hardware, capable of performing only if activated.

Figure 5-2   The first electronic digital computer, ENIAC. (*Courtesy of Sperry Corporation.*)

Operating System: Software which controls all of the hardware functions.

The basic functions of actually starting the automobile (hardware) or stopping it, causing it to turn right or left, etc., require the presence of an operator with the knowledge and capability to cause the automobile to perform. In this context, an automobile operator or driver may be compared to a computer's operating system. But even using this analogy, the mere presence of an operator, regardless of his or her knowledge and capacity to cause performance, still does not translate into reaching a desired destination.

Software: Programming or programs of all kinds.

In addition to the hardware (automobile) and operating system (driver), there must be a plan and a desire to travel. Such a plan can be very complex or very simple, depending

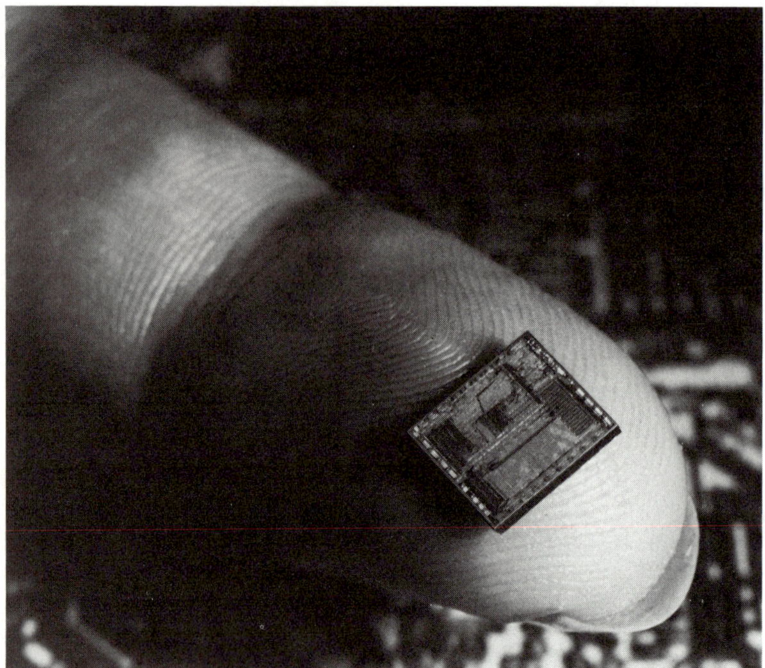

Figure 5-3   Intel's Silicone Chip, shown on the tip of a finger. (*Courtesy Intel Corporation.*)

upon distance and many other factors; however, it must be there in some form. The software, the plan and knowledge for reaching a destination, is an intangible, just as is the driver's operating knowledge. Taken individually, two or three components will not realize the goal or reach the destination; however, the combination of hardware, operator, and a program or plan will complete the necessary components, so that the functions can be carried out, and the desired destination reached. In a computer system, nearly everything other than the hardware itself is referred to as software; thus, *software* includes the operating system and any program applications to be performed.

What Is an Operating System?

We discussed the relationship of hardware, the operating system, and an application program; also that these components must all be present and coordinated. The operating system component generally functions much more independently of influence or intervention from the person using the computer than do the other two. With a microcomputer, the operating system may be read into the system when the equipment is turned on at the beginning of the day; it will not be of direct concern to the operator(s) again during the day, even though many different application programs may have functioned during that time. In very large computer systems, the operating system may rarely be turned off, day or night.

Programmer: Person who writes programs for a computer.

The purpose of the operating system is much like that of a traffic cop—to provide internal direction for the computer. This allows the programmer to spend his or her efforts on the problem or application requirements. As an example, when an item of data is input to the computer—for example, a keyboard key is depressed for a character to go into the computer's memory—neither the application programmer nor the operator wants to be concerned with which particular location in memory is to receive the character. However, these traffic decisions must be determined by some means and the actual placement carried out; this is performed by the operating system. Generally, the operating system will then wait for a confirmation that the placement was accurate; many such verifications are made by an operating system.

Thus it is that an application tells what is to be done, and the operating system directs the performance. Because the operating system can relieve the programmer of many very tedious and exacting steps, these operating systems have become very extensive and sophisticated. However, as stated before, the purpose of the operating system is to relieve the operator, in either word or data processing, of being aware of these internal directions and traffic.

A microcomputer consists of the obvious components such as keyboard, printer, and CRT; however, there are many internal components which are not so obvious. These components are described below.

- *RAM Memory* (Random-Access Memory): Storage or memory cells whose contents may be changed many times during processing at the direction of the program or the operator.

- *ROM Memory* (Read Only Memory): A portion of internal memory which cannot be altered once it leaves the manufacturer, and is used for special purposes, such as computer start-up.

- *Buffers:* Storage areas used to collect data in order to compensate for differences in rates of data flow, such as a printing buffer to hold print lines.

- *Registers:* An internal component capable of storing a specified amount of data or transferring that data very rapidly. Registers keep track of where we are in a program and where storage is available in memory.

- *Arithmetic/Logic Units:* The part of a processor containing the circuits that perform arithmetic and logical operations.

All of the external and internal components must be interconnected and interrelated, and all data movement and program instructions are controlled and carried out through the interrelationship of the software called the operating system.

One might ask how the operating system becomes part of the computer when it is first turned on, if all such movements are carried out by the operating system itself. The answer is that a particular type or portion of an operating system remains in that special type of internal computer memory called Read Only Memory (ROM) mentioned earlier. Certain ROM is always available to be accessed and the contents cannot be easily destroyed by writing over what was placed there when the computer was manufactured; nor are they lost when the computer is turned off. There are sufficient instructions in the ROM to insert the regular operating system into the Random Access Memory (RAM) when the computer is turned on. RAM, also mentioned earlier, is the dynamic memory of the computer, which is read to and written from repeatedly during processing.

As an analogy, everything perceived by your five senses finds its way to your memory cells. Your reaction or action depends upon your own mental program, which is also in your memory. A difference in the analogy, of course, is that you do not necessarily lose these mental images when you sleep, as the computer does when it is turned off.

There are several types and sizes of internal processors; however, there are many more brands of microcomputers than there are types of internal microprocessors (chips). The microprocessor is a hardware component where all data movement and processing logic are carried out. Microprocessors are extremely miniaturized and highly reliable. Generally, an operating system produced for a particular type of microprocessor can be used with any vendor brand of microcomputer encompassing that microprocessor.

Portable: The capability of using the data or programs created, used, or written for one equipment facility or another.

The first portable operating system for microcomputers, one that could easily be adapted to run on any computer having a particular processor, was CP/M, which stands for Control Program/Microcomputer, designed and marketed by Digital Research, Inc. in 1976. Versions of the CP/M operating system have been configured for a number of different microprocessors. This type of standardization allows the exchange of data, and to a degree, sets a standard for the production of application programs over a wide range of microcomputers.

It should be recognized, however, that other generalized operating systems have been developed by competing software organizations. Some of the better known ones are MS/DOS and PC/DOS by Microsoft, Inc.; UCSD, developed by the University of California at San Diego; and UNIX, developed by Bell Laboratories. These operating systems have also been configured for various microprocessors. While not restricted in any way, most microcomputer users will select one of the available operating systems for his or her system, and all of their applications will operate under that particular system.

What Is Application Software?

Commonly, software is portable; it exists on a diskette, external to the microcomputer or information processing hardware. As previously discussed, it is necessary that the operating system software be read and stored internally each time the computer is activated. Likewise, application software, whether it be word processing or data processing, must be read and stored in the computer's memory each time a new application program is to be processed. Upon completion of the tasks to be performed by one application program and the desire to use a different one, the new program is read and stored into memory for the next processing. At that time the operating system (software) remains in memory, and the application program (software) is replaced under control of the operating system. Frequently, the programs themselves cause other programs to be read into the computer, replacing what was there before. As you have learned, operating system software generally remains in memory until the computer is turned off.

Winchester Disk Drive: Original name given to hard disk drives.

In order to provide increased disk storage capacities, many vendors now offer the option of adding an internal hard disk, such as a Winchester disk drive. When an internal hard disk is used, the operating system and program software can reside there permanently; thus, reading these programs into memory becomes much easier and quicker. If the computer has been designed to handle one and only one function, like the earlier generations of word processing systems or certain computers used in manufacturing processes, both the operating system and application programs are highly integrated and permanently recorded into a machine component. In this instance—typical in the third generation of hardwired equipment—when the equipment was turned on, the software was already in place and operable.

Some processors, particularly those designed to function primarily as word processors, will have externally recorded software in which the operating system and application software are combined and integrated. Initiating the system in these cases involves insertion of only one software package via a diskette. An advantage of this arrangement is that the integration of the two allows processing efficiencies that could not be realized if they were separate; but a more significant advantage is that the operator is relieved of having to learn and deal with an operating system as such. Having to use operating system functions separately from the application to carry out certain steps can be both time consuming and complicated, depending upon the complexities of the operating system and the particular function being attempted. Performing word processing in this type of environment is common to microcomputers however, and is discussed later in this chapter.

What Is Data?

If hardware consists of the components that can be seen, touched, and identified, and software exists as logic embedded in a recorded medium, then what is data? Is it hardware, software?

Processing depends upon data for its functioning. Some programs process data item by item or group by group, as provided to the computer. This can be by various methods, such as an operator depressing a key or a communication being received; then the program waits either for more data or other instructions. However, the program remains activated until turned off or replaced. Other types of programs receive data in a file of some type, process it, and then come to the end of the job by their own instructions. In this case, the program can function again only by being restarted from the beginning. In a sense, data may be considered the fuel that causes the programs to proceed in either case.

Data can exist in many forms; some can be viewed directly, but to an increasing degree most exists in an electronic or magnetic state. However, regardless of the medium, data is rarely considered software; that designation usually refers only to the logic or programs under which the computer operates. Data is neither hardware nor software and is generally referred to solely as data.

The microcomputer's capability to fill office automation requirements has made it extremely popular among executives. The systems help with many daily tasks, allowing the executive to:

- Plot financial trends.
- Play "What if" with financial figures on electronic spreadsheets.
- Use voice/data services for telephone messaging.

- Keep a daily calendar of appointments.
- Communicate with a mainframe to access a data base.

The photograph in Figure 5–4 shows Sperry's Sperrylink Model 30 Desk Station with a spreadsheet program in process on the CRT. Though these application programs are helpful to executives, there are also applications which are used by support personnel, such as:

- Word processing—processing text information.
- Electronic mail—sending and receiving letters from an intelligent work station via communications.

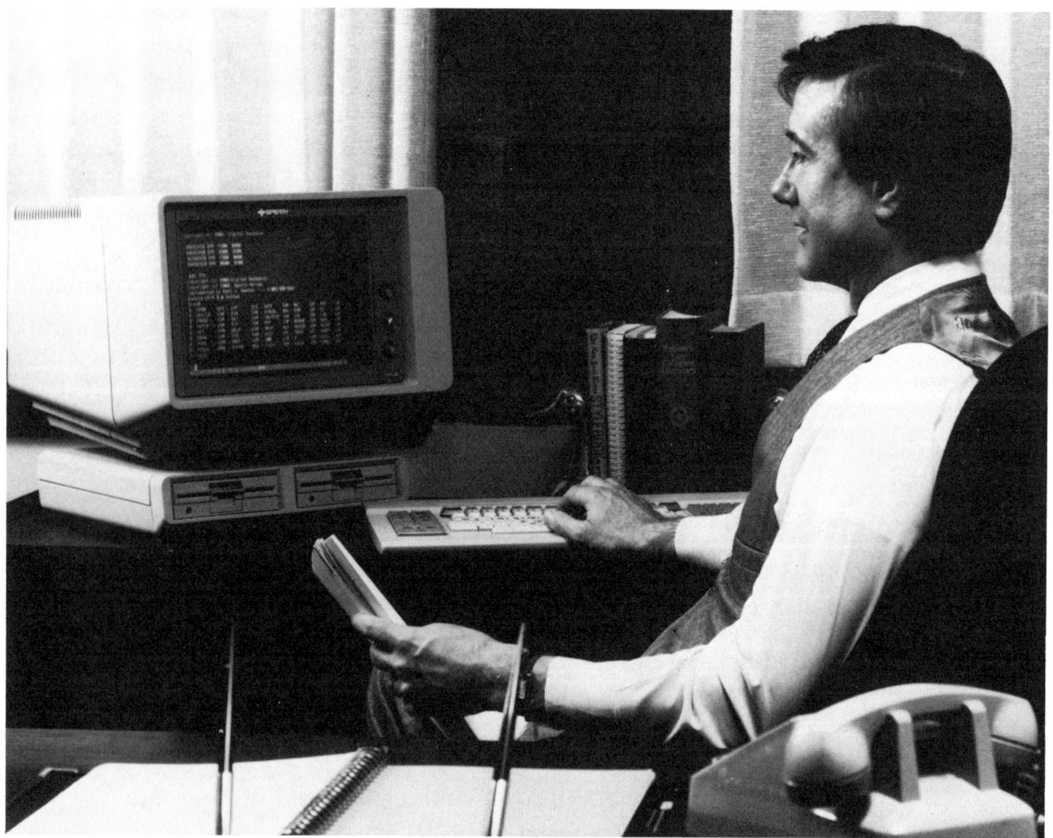

Figure 5-4   Sperry's SPERRYLINK Model 30 Desk Station. (*Courtesy Sperry Corporation Computer Systems.*)

- Communications—electronically transmitting messages and information without changing the sequence or content.
- Calendaring—future dates and events are placed in a file to allow the user to schedule time without conflicts.

The attraction of utilizing microcomputers in today's automated office lies in the ability of the operating system and suitable software to perform many different general applications. As we have learned, the same processor chip that is resident in microcomputers can also be found in dedicated word processing hardware. Further, as previously listed in the de facto standards for fourth generation software, data processing can also be accomplished on dedicated word processors. The major distinction is as follows:

- The CP/M, MS/DOS, PC/DOS, UNIX or UCSD-type operating systems for microcomputers can accept word processing software, or they can accept data processing.
- In a dedicated word processor, the word processing software and operating system are combined and integrated. In order to perform data processing applications, one of the above mentioned operating systems and program applications would be required. These are both available on diskettes.

"How," you might ask, "do we know which system to use?" The answer is directly related to function; word processors have dedicated function keys and supportive software which is solely to provide the efficiencies which support the de facto standards. This type of keyboard can be seen in Figure 5–5, which illustrates the dedicated function keys of a typical word processor. When word processing software is used on a microcomputer, the operator must use functions by pressing a control or command key of some type in conjunction with an alphabetic key or numbered function key. Typical of this type of keyboard is the IBM Personal Computer, illustrated in Figure 5–6. How the operator becomes involved with an operating

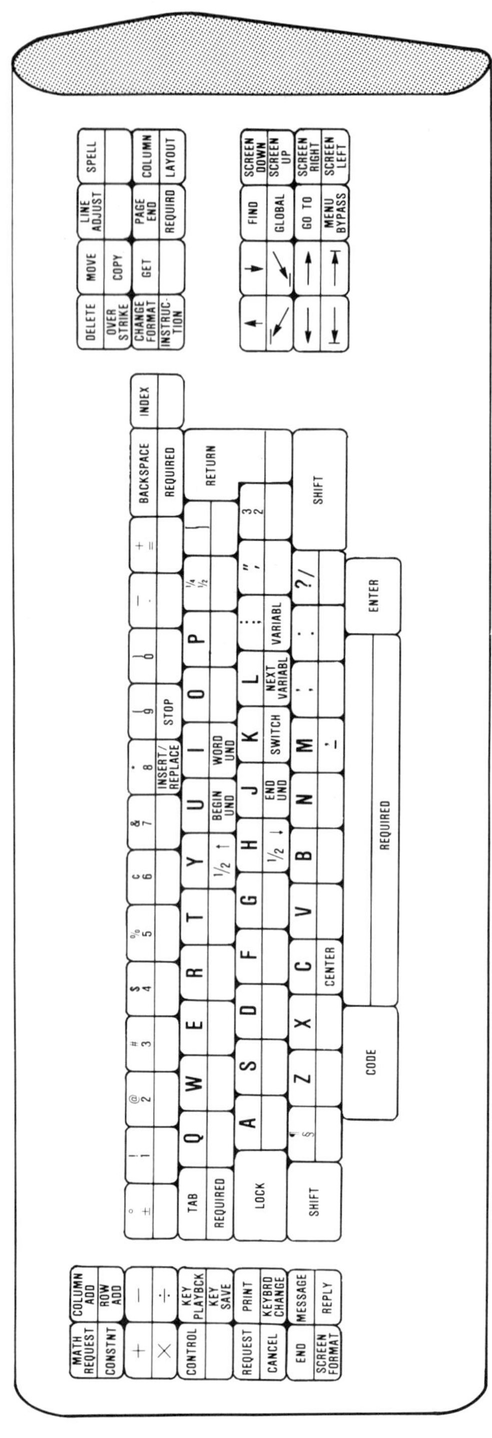

Figure 5-5 Typical Dedicated Word Processing Keyboard.

system when using word processing software, and the differences in functions, are discussed in the next section.

WORD PROCESSING (WP) SOFTWARE ON MICROCOMPUTERS

As we have learned, word processing software written to operate on microcomputers must accommodate the keyboard of the particular vendor's system. Some microcomputers have a row of programmable function keys across the top of the keyboard while others, such as the IBM PC, provide these types of keys

Figure 5.6(a)   The IBM PC. (*Courtesy IBM Corporation.*)

Figure 5-6(b)   The IBM PC Keyboard.

down either side of the keyboard (see Figure 5–6), while still others use alphabetic keys for functions. Whichever the case, functions are programmed to incorporate the particular vendor's keyboard. When the software is purchased, the user identifies the brand name of the computer or, if the software is sufficiently sophisticated, the user can tailor the software to accommodate the hardware. For example, the user can request that the key marked "F–1" will perform the insert mode. In order to know the functions of these unmarked keys, the operator uses a template to locate the software-supplied function (see Figure 5–7 illustrating the DisplayWrite word processing program's keyboard for the IBM PC).

As discussed in earlier chapters, the productivity that results from the presence of de facto standards, both software and hardware, is well documented. Achieving this productivity in a microcomputer environment, when utilizing an operating system and word processing application software, is somewhat more difficult, as additional keystrokes are required to accomplish a function. At times the operator will be required to exit the word processing software and interact with the operating system's utility programs, such as may be required when requesting the printing of a document. The hardware and software of microcomputers have other differences from the word processor, such as the location of cursor keys and their movement, insertion concepts, and memory capacities, to name a few. These differences between the dedicated word processing concepts and those of the microcomputer software are discussed in the following section.

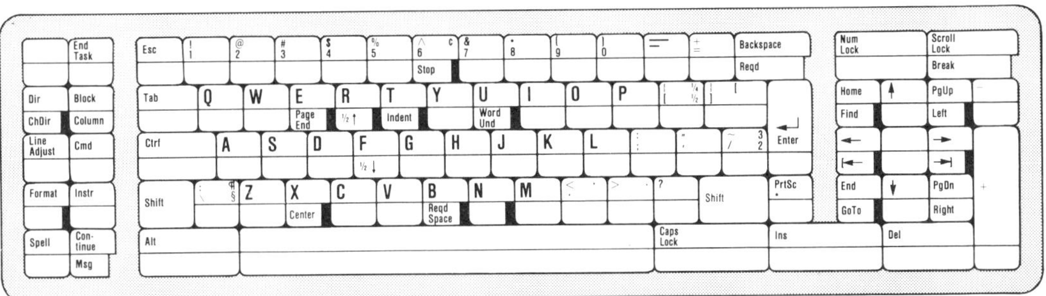

Figure 5-7   DisplayWrite 2 Keyboard for IBM PC.

Applying De Facto Standards to Applications

To make comparisons easier, Application 1 from Chapter 3 will be used again to evaluate the concepts of typical microcomputer WP software available. The specifications and task analysis for the document are repeated here for easier reference.

Application 1

DESCRIPTION

The project is composed of 60 pages of copy, a mixture of handwritten and typed pages. The subject matter deals with engineering and construction specifications, and there are numerous repetitive paragraphs.

The text is to be double spaced with some indented, single-spaced paragraphs, righthand justified, and printed in Letter Gothic at 12 pitch (12 characters per inch). Portions of the document will be used again to create new specifications.

TASK ANALYSIS PROCEDURE

In reviewing the document, it has been determined that its requirements are fairly uncomplicated, though it does incorporate a number of indented paragraphs when the engineering specifications occur. It appears that a great deal of time can be saved by keyboarding and storing the repetitive engineering specification paragraphs.

Since the document is partially typed, an investigation should be made to determine whether media exist, and if so, the location, so that the format of the original document can be analyzed for setup. Further examination should include the following:

- Is the material in a format to be removed easily with the format intact; that is, was the setup established according to the company's standards? Are the paragraphs to be copied scattered throughout the document?

- Is a hard copy available to determine the system page numbers, so that the needed material can be easily found?

- If not magnetically stored, are there enough typewritten pages of acceptable quality to use OCR input?

Use of Functions on a Microcomputer

Keyboarding

The document media could not be retrieved because of the prior operator's failure to document the earlier project; the project will be totally rekeyboarded.

Link: A method of combining documents during printing.

This document is 60 pages in length. In some microcomputer software, the maximum capacity for individual documents is only 17 pages. Additional pages must be divided into multiple documents or segments and "linked" together during the print function. In order to prepare for major revisions, the operator should allow enough unused space in each document for additional material. In this limited environment, insertions of any size would be assigned a document name by the operator, and then linked during printing.

Word processing software without a document size restriction provides much greater flexibility, as incorporating revisions is not a problem. However, many microcomputers, and most personal computers, use smaller disks which store an average of 75 pages. Documents exceeding this length will require more than one disk. As in the smaller segments of disk storage discussed above, an operator should not use more than three-fourths of a disk's space to allow for the possible movement of material.

Format

The original format of the document is double spaced. Since the indented, single-spaced format change is consistently the same, the format change is keyboarded once, stored in a phrase library or glossary, and then recalled when necessary. This procedure saves considerable time in recreating the format change. This concept is especially important when using microcomputer software, as more steps are required when format changes are not accomplished by dedicated function keys.

The insertion of the required format change in this application will probably involve the operator with the operating system, as changing margins is usually a function of the printing process. The operator will probably have to exit the word processing program and use the "PRINT" utility of the operating system. As previously discussed, the instructions for the CHANGE FORMAT would be given a name and stored in the phrase library for recall when necessary. The operator, once having established this format, would then re-enter the word processing program and continue keyboarding.

Paragraph Assembly

The standard paragraphs are stored in a library, just as they were with the dedicated word processing software. However, the "include" function has yet to be developed for this type of software. Though not a problem in this application of straight text, its absence would be noticed when attempting the MERGE function required in Application 3, discussed in Chapter 3.

Standard Document Disks

Since the originator has indicated that certain paragraphs will be used in future documents, a standard document diskette should be created containing those paragraphs. They can then be copied from disk to disk when required. If a hard disk is available on the system, standard material is best stored there for easy retrieval. In either case, a printout of standard recorded paragraphs should always be available for operators and originators of material.

Summary of Concepts

As stated earlier, standardization of documents is desirable for productive results. The standard page defaults vary between word processing software. Some concepts require that the page defaults be established with each document—that is, no overall defaults exist at all. Other software approaches allow users to establish their own defaults in the operating system. Documentation for this application can be found in Figure 5–8.

Some concepts to provide the de facto standards in microcomputer word processing software differ from the dedicated

```
┌─────────────────────────────────────────────────────────────────┐
│  SAMPLE DOCUMENT NO. 1                                           │
└─────────────────────────────────────────────────────────────────┘
```

Name of Document: No.1,2,3,4   **Date Document Created:** 9/15/YR

Type of Document: Engineering Specifications   **Originating Dept.:** Projects

Spacing: Double   **Typestyle:** Letter Gothic, 12 pitch

Margins: Left—18: Right—92

Disk Name: Spec1   **Disk Document Name:** Eng. Proj.50

Special Requirements: Document was created from Engineering Standards, Disk No.6. Remember to link documents before paginating.

Name of Keyboarding Person: Bill Pearson

DOCUMENTATION NOTES:

Figure 5-8 Documentation of procedures.

WP environment. Some of these different approaches are discussed in the following paragraphs.

Continuous Insert Mode

This type of insert is seldom available with microcomputer software. Specific keys at the top or side of the keyboard are designated as INSERT function keys and can have as many as three designations for insert. Examples of this would be insert during keyboarding, during the edit function, or for just one or two characters. Keyboard entry and edit (insert) modes are basic concepts that prevail in a computer environment.

There are trends in new WP software to reverse the requirement of two or more types of insert keys. In an analysis of the IBM DisplayWrite software, an observation was made that the screen editor was constantly in the insert mode, and that this concept was more effective.[3]

Full Cursor Movement

Full cursor movement is standard on typical software with the additional ability to advance by word, line, or paragraph. However, some keyboard configurations will cause cursor movement to be carried out using a series of alpha keys in conjunction with a code key.

Page Numbering

The method of accessing the page numbering function varies with microcomputer software, and is not always available.

Pagination and Spelling Checks

The average spelling verification dictionary contains 30,000 words. Additional words are created in supplemental dictionaries, and can be called up and applied to the document along with the main spelling verification. To use the spelling verification, the operator will probaby have to exit the word processing software and return to the operating system where a command is given to apply the spelling modules to a given document. With typical software, the spelling module scrolls through the

---

[3]John Dickinson, "IBM's DisplayWriter Begets a Family of PC Software," *PC Magazine,* 18 September, 1984, p. 240–241.

document and flags each word it does not recognize. When the operator types in the correct spelling, the corrected version may or may not appear on the screen; however, the correction does appear on the printed document.

Printing

Printing is a foreground activity with most microcomputer software, and no other activity can occur until document printing has been completed. When this concept is used for printing, productivity tends to suffer as the operator must wait for a document to print before working on any other project.

Microcomputer word processing software supports additional de facto standards that are important to specific applications and general operating requirements. The most common concept(s) for providing these standards are described in the following section.

Additional Microcomputer Functions

Automatic Footnote Control

This allows the system to remember where footnotes are to occur; the operator simply types them on the required page whenever he or she thinks of them. The system determines the spacing, allows for proper spacing at the end of the page, and remembers when the footnote is moved to a new page.

Recovery of Deleted Documents

Electronic Wastebasket: Term applied to a section on a disk designated by the software to record deleted material.

When a document is deleted, the disk directory will not list the document name. Most systems will still allow recovery by simply giving a command. Though not a formal electronic wastebasket, this capability can be most welcome when documents are inadvertently deleted.

Automatic Index

Though not previously discussed in dedicated WP de facto standards, this feature offers a function that could assist in text documentation. This feature provides for page identification and the alphabetizing of the information and is extremely helpful in building glossaries and indexes.

Disk Storage and Memory Capacity

Two other factors influence productivity when microcomputers are used for word processing: disk size and memory requirements of programs.

Disk Size

Density: The number of bits per inch of track on which information is recorded.

In addition to the document size limitations discussed in the previous exercise, where document size is predetermined, the limitations of disk storage capacity can also have a negative impact on productivity. Today's smaller mini (3.5″) and micro (5.25″) diameter disks have very limited storage when used in single density. However, dual density disks and disk drives are gaining in popularity as they store nearly double the number of characters on the recording surface of the disk. The difference between single and double density involves packing more bits per inch on a track, not increasing the number of tracks. Dual density disk drives will also record on both sides of a disk.

It is important to be aware of disk capacities in all information processing environments, as these limitations apply whether the hardware is a microcomputer or a dedicated word processor. For those systems that support the eight-inch, dual density disk drives, the user can anticipate a capacity of about 350 pages. When long documents are the rule rather than the exception, the eight-inch, dual density technology becomes a requirement. Quad density is now being offered by some vendors to ease the problems encountered in long document production.

Memory Capacity and Program Capability

K: In terms of data, a "K" of memory equals 1024 characters.

Memory limitations of a microcomputer become a factor when a particular program occupies all of the memory available. There are times when the addition of another program would increase productivity measurably. For example, when a document is being checked by the spelling verification function, the normal sequence would be to check hyphenation, to paginate, and to print the document at the same time. Small internal memory capacities, such as 64K, are inadequate to perform some of the more common multi-tasking functions required in a business environment. In home usage, on the other hand, where productivity is much less of a factor, the expenditure for a large system may be difficult to justify. Where multi-tasking and rapid program change are limited because of memory size, the primary penalty is usually a great deal more diskette or cassette handling and less sophisticated programs to perform the tasks.

The concerns of memory capacity and program demands are not necessarily discussed when acquiring or making a decision to use a particular brand of hardware or software. Processing decisions depend upon a thorough knowledge of a document's origin, paper path, and information destination for processing requirements. The concepts of software can have a positive or negative impact on productivity; those concepts and how they provide functions should be thoroughly investigated.

As discussed in the Introduction to this text, technological advances in information processing occur frequently. Personal computer (PC) manufacturers have recognized the productivity limitations of the computer-oriented keyboards and software, and WP keyboards are anticipated that will make PCs a more universal choice for information processing. Improvements to word processing software, plus the integration of programs, will probably deal a fatal blow to dedicated word processors in the second half of the 1980s.[4]

Word Processing Software Offerings by Vendor

Two major word processing vendors, IBM and NBI, have released versions of their word processing software to be run on the IBM PC. The NBI Word Processing (see Figure 5–9) and the IBM DisplayWrite 2 and 3 represent the first software version from the dedicated word processors for the PC environment.

We include a list of vendors who provide word processing software for microcomputers in order to provide knowledge of the industry, as well as to serve as a resource (see Figure 5–10). As previously stated, staying abreast of technology advances and offerings is most difficult, as new offerings and editions of

---

[4]*The Seybold Report on Office Systems,* 1 January 1985, Vol. 8, No. 1, p. 17.

Figure 5-9   NBI word processing software for IBM® PC. (*Courtesy of NBI Corporation.*)

hardware and software are daily occurrences. However, just as representative industry vendors of dedicated word processing were listed in Chapter 1, the list of microcomputer-oriented word processing software vendors can serve as reference for future and current users. The list is by no means complete, but is rather a random sampling of software available, noting the vendor and software name, general description of the functions available, and the name of the appropriate operating system required to run the software.

Integrated Software

Two major technological advances have impacted the usefulness of word processing programs on microcomputers: windowing and integrated software.

When using a word processing program, you have no

Figure 5-10   Vendors of Microcomputer word processing software.

Vendor	*Name of Software*	*Operating System*
Apple Computer, Inc. Cupetino, CA	Apple Writer • Text Processing	SOS
IBM Armonk, NY	DisplayWrite 2 and 3 • Text editing, named variable merge, auto pagination, integrated spell checking, column processing and math. Equivalent to Textpack 4 and 6, respectively	PCDOS®
Information Unlimited Software, Inc. Sausalito, CA	EasyWriter II • Text editing	MSDOS®
Lexisoft, Inc.	Spellbinder • Text editing, font tracking, spelling verification	CP/M-86® or Concurrent CP/M-86®
Leading Edge Products, Inc. Canton, MA	Leading Edge Word Processing • Text Processing	
Lifetree Software, Inc. Monterey, CA	Volswriter Delux	PCDOS
Mark of the Unicorn Arlington, MA	FinalWord • Text editing, split screen/windowing, automatic outline, merge/list processing check, phrase library	
MicroPro International San Rafael, CA	WordStar® • Text editing • MailMerge • SpellStar • StarIndex	CP/M®, CP/M-86®, MP/M®, IBM PC-DOS®, MSDOS®, Apple with CP/M® option

Figure 5-10   *(continued)*

Vendor	*Name of Software*	*Operating System*
Monroe Systems for Business Morris Plains, NJ	SuperWord® • Text editing, merge options, paragraph assembly • SuperMerge	CP/M®
NBI Boulder, Colorado	NBI Word Processing Program • Text editing, auto outline, merge auto hyphenation, paragraph assembly, menu-driven	Special Plug-in Board
Office Solutions, Inc. Madison, WI	OfficeWriter	PCDOS
Onyx Systems, Inc. San Jose, CA	ONtext • Text editing, menu-driven, "Wang-like" word processing, split windows	UNIX®
Peachtree Software Atlanta, GA	Magic Wand Word Processing • Text editing, merge • Mail Merge • Spell Star	CP/M®
R & B Computer System Tempe, AZ	The Benchmark • Text editing	North Star DOS®
Satellite Software International Orem, Utah	WordPerfect • Text editing, list processing, math, hyphenation, paragraph assembly, draw lines	
Software Publishing Co. Mountain View, CA	Pfs:Write	IBM PCDOS, Apple

Softword Systems, Inc.	MultiMate • Text editing, background printing, library, math	PCDOS®
Structured Systems Group, Inc. Oakland, CA	Word Right • Text editing, merge, hyphenation	CP/M-86®
Vector Graphics, Inc. Thousand Oaks, CA	Memorite III • Text editing, mail list and merge, spelling	CP/M-80® Concurrent CP/M-86®
VisiCorp San Jose, CA	VisiWord • Text editing, menu-oriented	PCDOS®

doubt experienced the need or desire to view another document without changing the screen you were currently viewing. By using an operating system that allows for the integration of programs, a user can view another word processing document, the results of a spreadsheet, the contents of a data base, or perhaps their electronic mail.

This capability is called "windowing"; the operator simply requests the information desired by identifying it by name, and the information will appear in a small area on the screen, or in a window. Information processing firms—IBM, Apple, and Microsoft, to name a few—have opened the door to major developments in this area with their individual versions of this type of software. Information processing forecasters predict that in the near future, all operating systems will allow for this type of integration.

Copyright Laws for Software

Software can be described as the written instructions that are given to a computer. These instructions are written in programming language and are resident on some type of magnetic media. The operating system and applications software are the result of someone's original work and effort, and as such are protected by the United States Constitution and the Copyright Laws. This protection prohibits the duplicating, or copying, of the software media for the purpose of selling it to a third party. Duplicating the original software is permitted only for the convenience of the user. When software is purchased, the buyer signs a written agreement to abide by these restrictions. Though the opportunity to duplicate program software may be tempting, the act is punishable by law and carries significant penalties.

Using Minicomputers for Information Processing

In the hierarchy of computers, the minicomputer ranks in the middle-sized classification—between micros and mainframes. A typical minicomputer system would support anywhere from 1 to 36 terminals, or a combination of terminals, printers, and other communicating devices.

The minicomputer system will offer the full range of integrated processing: data processing, word processing (text management), communications, office administration, and business graphics. Because of this wide range of function, the user will find a more restricted environment. Depending upon their jobs, users may be limited to the functions and information that they are allowed to use. The word/information processing environment of such a system is discussed in the following section.

Text Management

Text management, another term for word processing, on minicomputeres has traditionally been poor compared to the advances of standalone word processors. However, as the industry has matured, and the demand for integrated processing has increased, standard functions have begun to reflect the more sophisticated word processing de facto standards.

For example, IBM's System/36 offers the same word processing that was resident on the DisplayWriter, their popular standalone that set the industry de facto standards in the early 1980s, in an integrated system.

Most of these integrated systems use menus to guide the user from text entry through the printing process; consequently, there is little interaction with the operating system. A typical text management program will incorporate the following procedures:

Library: (see Glossary)

- Daily signing in and off of the system through a user ID/password.
- Through a series of menus, access the Text Management program.
- Create, store and retrieve documents through a specific library of programs.
- Use on-line tutorial systems.
- Access standard documents that are identified with your particular ID password.
- Access a variety of printers for draft or final copy. For example: *Line printers* (draft) that print up to 560 lines per minute (lpm), plotters for graphics, dot matrix printers with speeds up to 240 lpm, and letter quality, impact printers with sheet feeders.

Integrated Processing

The keyboard of an integrated processing system is computer oriented, and will be similar to that of a PC as described earlier in this chapter. All text management functions, such as *move, delete, copy,* etc. are accomplished through a set of existing numbered keys. (See Figure 5–6 for similar keyboard.) Though a user cleared to utilize text management may never have the opportunity or requirement to use the other features of the system, he or she needs to know what types of programs are on the computer. Typical programs found on an integrated system are discussed below.

Data Processing

The data processing programs resident are limited only to the needs of the particular organization. At this level of computer, the hardware manufacturer offers a substantial amount of software for full accounting, inventory, payroll, personnel records, etc.

Administrative Management Systems

Integrated processing provides a variety of management tools, such as calendaring, handling incoming and outgoing mail, updating telephone lists, graphics creation and printing, and word processing. The word processing system may be less sophisticated than found in the text management system.

Programming Aids

Users can usually program in a variety of languages, and have access to compilers and editors from their terminals.

Security

Security for the system can be provided at a number of levels. For example, security is established at the primary level by requiring the operator to enter his or her password before access to the system is allowed. Further restrictions are pre-established via limited access to files and libraries according to user IDs. Additional restrictions are placed upon users through limiting their menu access.

Communications

Multiple communication functions for direct, interactive, and remote connections as well as local connections to other intelligent systems, such as OCR readers, printers, PCs, standalone word processors, telex or facsimile copiers.

This text does not attempt to evaluate integrated systems nor establish standards, as a thorough knowledge of computer systems architecture would be a prerequisite to such an analysis. However, from a user standpoint, it is valuable to understand that integrated office automation technology is being attempted through a number of concepts: standalone systems communicating via telecommunications and LANs, information processing systems using multiple terminals and communications for all OA except centralized data processing, and integrated office systems incorporating minicomputers to provide all OA function. All three environments offer their own unique user benefits and inhibitors to productivity.

The use of communications to achieve integrated processing is the subject of the next chapter.

DISCUSSION QUESTIONS

1. List the three major processes in computer function.
2. What is the function of an operating system?

3. When is the word processing operating system loaded on dedicated word processors?

4. What problems occurred in the keyboarding of Document 1?

5. If you are currently training on a word/information processor, compare the spelling verification concepts of that system to that of the microcomputer spelling verification.

6. What is the major difference between the keyboards of microcomputers and dedicated word processors?

7. How do copyright laws affect software?

8. Compare document security systems found in stand-alones and computers.

6

Data Communications

Once information or data has been gathered and stored electronically, its usefulness is measured by its timely distribution to those whose continued work or decision making is dependent upon receiving it. Once information reaches its destination, it must be in a form to meet the user's needs. In this era, when information can be an organization's most valuable asset, business and industry rely upon communication to distribute information efficiently from one point to another, whether internally or externally.

In an imaginative incorporation of state-of-the-art office automation and communication technologies, the 1984 Summer Olympic Games in Los Angeles, through the cooperative effort of corporate sponsors, established communication links among some 50,000 officials, staff, journalists, athletes, and coaches who participated in an area of over 4,500 square miles. The technologies that merged to provide this total information network system included American Telephone and Telegraph—telecommunications and computer equipment; International Business Machines—office systems and voice messaging systems; MCI International—telex messaging terminals and services; Motorola—pagers, portable radio equipment, and cellular radio-telephones; Pacific Bell—fiber optic telephone and data communications cables; and Xerox Corporation—copiers, facsimile terminals, and electronic equipment.[1] This Olympian-like effort incorporated many different technologies, combined to enhance the ability to communicate. As discussed in the introduction of this text, word processing hardware is often the sender and receiver of information to be used in other word processing environments or to be processed by other intelligent machines. The steps in providing this type of communication are examined in the following discussion.

In a business office, it is often necessary to share previously stored information with other locations. This information

---

[1] "Extraordinary Communications at the Olympics," *Office Administration and Automation,* June 1984, p. 62–63.

might be a client mailing list stored on a computer, a multi-page report, stored on a word processor, that needs to be typeset; a legal document that requires revision by a lawyer in a distant city; or one of the many applications of word processing. Though it is possible to send paper images of documents electronically (to be discussed in Chapter 7), our discussion here will look at the ways in which word processing hardware and software provide for communicating information which has been electronically stored.

Telecommunications: Distribution of information via telephone lines, telegraph, radio.

The two most common methods of electronic communication on a dedicated word processor are *telecommunications* and *local area networks (LANs)*. Both types of communication provide information distribution without changing or altering the information.[2]

Local Area Networks (LANs): The direct interconnection of computerized equipment by cables or wires for the interchange of processing throughout the network.

Communicating information by telecommunication or LAN systems fulfills the need to share or transfer information, whether to similar or dissimilar devices. Communication can be viewed as the glue that holds office automation together, the binding ingredient that allows information to be shared. Typical of a fourth generation word/information processing system that provides this type of communication is the Wang OIS 40 and 50 shown in Figure 6-1. The system features data communication, electronic mail (MAILWAY), and local area networking. The demand for the transfer of information through communications is also developing outside the traditional office. The hotel industry, in an attempt to attract more business, is placing PCs equipped with communications in hotel rooms. The more innovative hotels allow guests to communicate with their offices, to create documents, and to receive information on the stock market, airline schedules, and entertainment.[3]

COMPATIBILITY BETWEEN SYSTEMS

Communication to like vendor equipment is usually a simple matter of making a few choices from a menu on the word proc-

---

[2]Marilyn Bohl, *Information Processing* 4th ed. (Chicago: Science Research Associates, Inc., 1984), p. 475.

[3]*Information Industry Review*, Newsletter of the Association of Information Systems Professionals, November/December 1984, p. 2.

Figure 6-1   Wang OIS 40 and OIS 50 in office setting. (*Courtesy Wang Corporation.*)

essor, as the systems are compatible for the exchange of information. However, when communicating with differing vendor equipment or differing technologies, the systems cannot recognize one another without changing various parameters so that they can talk to each other in the same language.

Communications software and hardware in dedicated word processors has, to a degree, created compatibility among some systems; however, without communication capability, compatibility would not exist. Though vendors claim "IBM compatibility" or "Wang compatibility," etc., it does not mean that the end result of the communication effort will be "clean." In attempts to communicate from one intelligent device to another it is often the case that the received document or information is in a different format and requires considerable

Soft Carriage Return (SCR): Term for cursor automatic return to left margin during keyboarding.

Hard Carriage Return (HCR): Results when the carriage return is pressed.

"clean-up" to recreate the document's original image. This incompatibility can be compared to a language barrier.

This language barrier occurs, for example, if machine brand A uses one programming code for a soft carriage return while brand B uses the identical code for a hard carriage return. In this instance, when the transmission is complete and editing of the document is attempted, the operator will find hard carriage returns at the end of each line, making the auto wordwrap feature inoperative. The most common problem experienced in communications between dedicated word processors is this failure to recognize codes, such as tab settings, center instructions, or format changes. When these inconsistencies are minor, the de facto function of GLOBAL SEARCH AND REPLACE can assist in the "cleanup" of these errors. There are times when only deleting incorrect codes and inserting correct codes will correct the errors.

When word processors communicate with data processing equipment, problems are encountered in the concept of field size, because in data processing, field lengths are usually fixed. In word processing, the systems usually allow for flexibility in field size. In addition, data processing fields use spaces to serve as field markers, where word processors tend to use tabs or carriage returns. Though the American National Standards Institute (ANSI) has begun work on the formation of text structure that would begin an exchange of character codes,[4] no two word processors have compatible recording of functions. Unfortunately, for many multi-vendor installations who had planned on utilizing communications to exchange information, realization of incompatibility comes too late.

Multi-vendor installations evolve for a number of reasons. Typical is the installation that chooses to retain old systems for particular applications while acquiring new generations of equipment for other applications.[5] This situation most often occurs when the various departments within a firm make their own equipment decisions, only later identifying additional ap-

---

[4]Bryan Williams, "Office Systems Standards Are Going Forward," *MIS Week*, Feb. 22, 1984.

[5]Paula F. Calise and Mary E. Locke, "Coping with Multivendor Installations," *Words, the Journal of the Association of Information Systems Professionals*, Aug.-Sept., 1983, p. 34–36.

plications where sharing of data would be helpful. Unfortunately, total compatibility between dedicated word processors does not exist. As previously discussed, each dedicated word processor has its own operating system and software, and only disks recorded under that software will be recognized by the system. Communication is the most effective method of bringing about some measure of compatibility, or recognition of other systems.

BASICS OF COMMUNICATIONS

Before any telecommunications can take place, the hardware must be equipped with the proper communications software, a dedicated telephone line must be installed, and the proper modem must be connected between the telephone system and the hardware. As we have discussed, word processors have the ability to communicate with intelligent machines other than word processors, including computers, copiers, microcomputers, OCR equipment, and typesetting composers. Though most of these electronic devices have the ability to communicate, their dissimilarities can cause major stumbling blocks when attempting to send information or to have these devices "talk" to each other. This difficulty can be compared to two persons, speaking different languages, who are engaged in a telephone conversation; the telephone works, but they cannot understand one another. These difficulties lie in the basic parameters established when the device was manufactured, and should be addressed when considering communication applications.

Word processing hardware vendors, for the most part, offer IBM communication parameters, as vendors have come to realize the importance of being able to co-exist in an IBM environment. This is primarily because of the large IBM-installed computer base. The presence of EBCDIC, 2741 (IBM host computers), and other IBM compatibility codes in communications software reflects this reality. In order to bring about successful communication links, however, the operator must choose the proper options prior to the actual communication attempt. The following section describes those options and provides sample documentation, which is recommended procedure following successful communications.

Preset Parameters of Communications

Depending upon the brand of word processing equipment and its accompanying software, certain parameters are preset that designate the type of modem that must be used. The modem regulates the speed of the transmission, which in turn is dependent upon the mode of transmissions chosen by the manufacturer. Also, the manufacturer has used either ASCII or EBCDIC code in its software. These parameters are described below.

- Modem: Translates the digital signals of an information processor into analog, or voice-type, signals for telephone transmission. Similar modems must be installed at sending and receiving locations to allow for this process, called modulation/demodulation. The digital signal is modulated or changed into an analog signal acceptable for telephone transmission. When the signal is received at the remote location, it must be demodulated back into its original form. The term MODEM is an acronym describing this function. Designations on modems refer to *baud rates* defined by bits per second of transmission, or how fast they communicate. Lower speeds generally support asynchronous transmission, with higher rates supporting binary synchronous; some support both. Both sending and receiving modems must be at the same baud rate.

- Codes: *ASCII (American Standard Code for Information Interchange)*—seven-bit code, or *EBCDIC (Extended Binary Coded Decimal Interchange Code)*—eight-bit code (most common) in IBM equipment.

- Mode of Transmission: *Asynchronous*—blocks or groups of characters are transmitted with stop and start signals, or *Binary Synchronous (bisynchronous)*—a constant time interval exists between bits or characters during transmittal.

- Direction of Transmission: *Half-Duplex*—sending or receiving capability, but only one direction at a time. *Full-Duplex*—sending or receiving capability, simultaneously.
- Dedicated Telephone Line: Dedicated telephone lines are advised for telecommunications to avoid interruption. When a rotary line is used, an incoming call can interrupt data communications. Similar problems are caused when modems are attached to home telephones equipped with a call-waiting capability; an incoming call will interrupt and disconnect data communications.

Rotary Line: When the first is busy, the next incoming call moves to the next line.

Applying Communications

With an understanding that a matching of all the communication parameters between systems must be achieved before successful transmission of communications can take place, we will examine in more detail the steps involved. Basically, there are two communication modes:

Interactive communication, such as at airline ticket counters where knowledge of the most recent activity of reservations is a requirement. In this example, the reservation information is constantly updated through communications, and information flows in two directions, from the operator to the computer, and from the computer to the operator's screen, simultaneously.

Batch communication, such as a word processing center sending a document or documents to another location. In this instance, the document to be sent is called up by the operator, the receiving location's telephone number is dialed, and once the connection is made, all documents are sent without interruption.

It is possible, on some systems, to be in a "conversational" mode, which allows the operators of the two systems to talk to one another via the CRT screen.

Setting Up Communications

In order to conclude successful communications, certain parameters must be considered and mirrored at each station, much the same way that margins and space requirements are made in menu selections prior to keyboarding.

When setting up a communication session, as previously discussed, standards and options must be designated by the operators at each end of the planned communications link. These decisions assist the system in establishing the correct parameters that identify the receiving terminal and enable the information to be received in a readable and usable format. The following parameters are most likely to be found on a communications menu.

- *Protocol:* Specifies rules for transmitting information.
- *Options:* Describes the type of communication, e.g., IBM CMC (communicating mag card), TTY (teletypewriter-like products, or host computers), 2741 (IBM host computers).
- *Keyboard ID:* The keyboards must match, i.e., 88- or 96-character keyboards, plus over 50 optional keyboards.
- *Line Speed:* Baud rate of modem being used.
- *EOT Disconnect:* Asks whether disconnect should be automatic when an EOT (End of Transmission) is received.
- *Echoplex:* Allows data being transmitted to be displayed on the receiving CRT for verification.
- *Parity:* Type of error checking.

Documenting Communication Setups

Since setting up for communications requires a number of decisions, it is important to document the procedures once the proper options have been determined, just as it was important to document the procedures in keyboarding discussed in Chapters 3 and 5. Some software provides an internal method of storing the setup for future recall, in which case the documentation should also include the reference or name given to the stored setup. For additional assistance to the operator at the receiving location, the following information can be communicated first:

- Date of communication
- Document ID (Identifying Code)
- Sender's ID
- Sender's telephone number

The communication parameters of IBM DisplayWriter have been chosen for the originating word processor in the following examples, as most other systems are designed to communicate with IBM protocols. Documentation for the examples can be found in Figures 6–2 through 6–5. A variety of receiving equipment has been used to illustrate the many applications for communicating word processing documents.

Applying Communications

COMMUNICATION SESSION 1

The first example details an IBM DisplayWriter communicating to a Sony series 35 word processor. The setup requires asynchronous communication. (See Figure 6–2 for documentation.) Note that the baud line speed of 1200 is at the upper level for asynchronous communications.

COMMUNICATION SESSION 2

The Compugraphic Phototypesetter is receiving a financial document in this example (see Figure 6–3). This particular document is a firm's year-end financial statement, composed of many pages. Once all of the figures were typed, the information was communicated to the Compugraphic to be typeset and printed for inclusion in an annual report. For more information concerning typesetters, see Chapter 7.

COMMUNICATION SESSION 3

An IBM DisplayWriter communicating to IBM Personal Computer is shown in this example. This type of communications application will most likely occur when a PC is at a location where data processing applications are prevalent and there is a need to include some of this information in a word processing document. Documentation for this example is in Figure 6–4.

ID ITEM	YOUR CHOICE	POSSIBLE CHOICES
a Setup Name	Sony	Up to ten letters or more
b Protocol	3	1 = IBM CMC 2 = 2741 3 = TTY
c Highlight Received Data	2	1 = yes 2 = no
COMMUNICATIONS SETUP		
a Line Speed	5	1 = 110 2 = 150 3 = 200 4 = 300 5 = 1200
b Inactivity Disconnect	2	1 = yes 2 = no
c EOT Disconnect	2	1 = yes 2 = no
d Echoplex	2	1 = yes 2 = no
e Parity	1	1 = even 2 = odd 3 = none
f Terminal ID		
g Automatic Answerback	2	1 = yes 2 = no
h Change Extended Options		0 = none 1 = TTY 2 = 2741 3 = CMC
TTY OPTIONS		
a Send New Line	1	1 = CR LF 2 = CR 3 = LF 4 = XOFF 5 = CR XOFF
b Display Send New Line	1	1 = New Line 2 = CR 3 = LF 4 = None
c Receive as New Line	1	1 = CR LF 2 = CR 3 = LF 4 = XOFF
d Send Pacing	1	1 = None 2 = Stop at Line End, Wait for XON 3 = Stop when XOFF Received, Wait for XON
2741 OPTIONS		
a Line Speed		1 = 134.5 2 = 300 3 = 1200
b Inactivity Disconnect		1 = yes 2 = no
c Send All Codes		1 = yes 2 = no
d Terminal ID		Up to four characters
CMC OPTIONS		
a Line Speed		1 = 134.5 2 = 300 3 = 1200
b Inactivity Disconnect		1 = yes 2 = no
NOTES:		

Figure 6-2 Asynchronous communications documentation IBM Displaywriter to Sony series 35.

DEFINE SETUP

ID	ITEM	YOUR CHOICE	POSSIBLE CHOICES
a	Setup Name	Compu	Up to ten letters or numbers
b	Protocol	1	1=2770/3780 2=2780
c	Send Format	2	1=Card Image
			2=Page Image Text Only
			3=Page Image with OCL
			4=Page with Format Line
			5=Media Image
			6=Select on Job Basis

Next Screen:

COMMUNICATION SETUP

ID	ITEM	YOUR CHOICE	POSSIBLE CHOICES		
a	Modem Port	1	1=Port 4	2=Port 4A	3=Port 4B
b	Primary	2	1=Yes	2=No	
c	Block Size	3	1=128	2=256	3=512
d	CPU Mode	2	1=yes	2=no	
e	Insert New Line Codes	2	1=yes	2=no	
f	Transparency	2	1=yes	2=no	
g	Code Set	1	1=EBCDIC	2=7 Bit	
h	Change Setup Session Options (Choose "h" and an additional screen appears: a=1; b=2; c=1; d=2; e=2; f=2; g=2; h=2				
i	Create or Revise Session ID's				

Next Screen:

CHANGE SETUP SESSION OPTIONS

ID	ITEM	YOUR CHOICE	POSSIBLE CHOICES	
a	Keyboard ID		1-999	
b	Use this Keyboard ID for all send documents		1=yes	2=no
c	Receive Default Format		1=Your Document Default Format	
			2=Your Alternate Default Format	
d	Delete Send Queue Entry After Sending		1=yes	2=no
e	Send Document Messages		1=yes	2=no
f	6670 Print Options		1=yes	2=no
g	Append Next Document		1=Select on Job Basis	
			2=no	
h	Wait for Response		1=Select on Job Basis	
			2=no	

CREATE OR REVISE SESSION ID'S

Next Screen

ID	ITEM	YOUR CHOICE
a	Local ID	
b	Remote ID 1	
c	Remote ID 2	
d	Remote ID 3	
e	Remote ID 4	

SPECIAL NOTES/INFORMATION:

For this session always send translation table (typesetter codes) before sending document.

Figure 6-3   Bisynchronous communications documentation, IBM Displaywriter to Compugraphic.

DEFINE SETUP			
ID	**ITEM**	**YOUR CHOICE**	**POSSIBLE CHOICES**
a	Setup Name	PC	Up to 10 letters or more
b	Protocol	3	1 = IBM CMC 2 = 2741 3 = TTY
c	Highlight Received Data	2	1 = yes 2 = no

COMMUNICATIONS SETUP			
a	Line Speed	5	1 = 110 2 = 150 3 = 200 4 = 300 5 = 1200
b	Inactivity Disconnect	2	1 = yes 2 = no
c	EOT Disconnect	2	1 = yes 2 = no
d	Echoplex	2	1 = yes 2 = no
e	Parity	1	1 = even 2 = odd 3 = none
f	Terminal ID		
g	Automatic Answerback	2	1 = yes 2 = no
h	Change Extended Options	0 = none	1 = TTY 2 = 2741 3 = CMC

TTY OPTIONS			
a	Send New Line	1	1 = CR LF 2 = CR 3 = LF 4 = XOFF 5 = CR XOFF
b	Display Send New Line	1	1 = New Line 2 = CR 3 = LF 4 = None
c	Receive as New Line	1	1 = CR LF 2 = CR 3 = LF 4 = XOFF

d	Send Pacing	1	1 = None
			2 = Stop at Line End,
			    Wait for XON
			3 = Stop when XOFF Received,
			    Wait for XON

2741 OPTIONS			
ID	**ITEM**	**YOUR CHOICE**	**POSSIBLE CHOICES**
a	Line Speed		1 = 134.5 2 = 300 3 = 1200
b	Inactivity Disconnect		1 = yes 2 = no
c	Send All Codes		1 = yes 2 = no
d	Terminal ID		Up to four characters

CMC OPTIONS			
ID	**ITEM**	**YOUR CHOICE**	**POSSIBLE CHOICES**
a	Line Speed		1 = 134.5 2 = 300 3 = 1200
b	Inactivity Disconnect		1 = yes 2 = no

NOTES:

Figure 6-4   Asynchronous communications documentation, IBM Displaywriter to IBM PC.

<table>
<tr><td colspan="3" align="center">DEFINE SETUP</td></tr>
<tr><td>ID ITEM</td><td>YOUR CHOICE</td><td>POSSIBLE CHOICES</td></tr>
<tr><td>a Setup Name</td><td>Shaffstall</td><td>Up to ten letters or numbers</td></tr>
<tr><td>b Protocol</td><td>2</td><td>1=2770/3780   2=2780</td></tr>
<tr><td>c Send Format</td><td>2</td><td>1=Card Image
2=Page Image Text Only
3=Page Image with OCL
4=Page with Format Line
5=Media Image
6=Select on Job Basis</td></tr>
</table>

Next Screen:

COMMUNICATION SETUP

ID ITEM	YOUR CHOICE	POSSIBLE CHOICES		
a Modem Port	1	1=Port 4	2=Port 4A	3=Port 4B
b Primary	2	1=Yes	2=No	
c Block Size	2	1=128	2=256	3=512
d CPU Mode	2	1=yes	2=no	
e Insert New Line Codes	2	1=yes	2=no	
f Transparency	2	1=yes	2=no	
g Code Set	1	1=EBCDIC	2=7 Bit	
h Change Setup Session Options				
i Create or Revise Session ID's				

Next Screen:

CHANGE SETUP SESSION OPTIONS

ID ITEM	YOUR CHOICE	POSSIBLE CHOICES	
a Keyboard ID		1-999	
b Use this Keyboard ID for all send documents		1=yes	2=no
c Receive Default Format		1=Your Document Default Format 2=Your Alternate Default Format	
d Delete Send Queue Entry After Sending		1=yes	2=no
e Send Document Messages		1=yes	2=no
f 6670 Print Options		1=yes	2=no
g Append Next Document		1=Select on Job Basis 2=no	
h Wait for Response		1=Select on Job Basis 2=no	

CREATE OR REVISE SESSION ID'S

Next Screen

ID ITEM	YOUR CHOICE
a Local ID	
b Remote ID 1	
c Remote ID 2	
d Remote ID 3	
e Remote ID 4	

SPECIAL NOTES/INFORMATION:

For this session always send translation table (typesetter codes) before sending document.

Figure 6-5 Bisynchronous communications documentation, IBM Displaywriter to Bedford Phototypesetter via Shaffstall.

COMMUNICATION SESSION 4

Here the Displaywriter is communicating to a Bedford Photo-typesetter. However, since the Bedford does not read IBM Displaywriter code, the communication is first received by a Shaftstall language converter, which in turn completes the communication to the phototypesetter. As discussed in Chapter 7, the Shaftstall also serves as a media conversion tool. Documentation for this example can be found in Figure 6–5.

Local Area Network (LAN) Communications

In the previous section, we looked at telecommunications which are most often used in communicating over long distances. Telecommunications can also be used within a single office complex; however, since telecommunications require a dedicated telephone line and modem at each station, it is considered too costly for large, in-house installations. Further, this type of communication does not allow for the sharing of peripheral devices. A local area network (LAN) can be described as a system to transmit information or data to two or more points simultaneously within a relatively small area, or within a building or group of buildings. Put another way, a LAN system is a communication capability that does not incorporate common carriers or public communications facilities. For example, a small computer can serve as a controller or traffic director, allowing word processors, copiers, facsimile machines, OCR readers, printers, and intelligent work stations to share information. An example of a single vendor system can be seen in Figure 6–6, the Burroughs Office Information System. This system connects word processors, computers, copiers, and various other information processing equipment.

The development of LANs was brought about by the proliferation of microcomputers in the office environment. Once users of these desktop computers became accustomed to the computing power, they requested additional functions, such as the sharing of information from data bases, using a variety of printers, and sharing of information from word processing documents. The desire for sharing between different technologies required a new kind of communication, as these intelligent machines could not talk to each other. The end result was a

Figure 6-6 Burroughs' OFIS 1. (*Courtesy Burrough's Corporation.*)

method of information exchange to truly support office automation.

LANs are supplied by either: (1) the major communication, computer, and word processing hardware vendors to provide the technology for their own equipment, called proprietary, or (2) individual vendors in the communications industry who provide supporting products, termed independent. As protocol standards for the industry will be emerging over a period of time, vendors will select from a variety of options to create a network architecture, or the pathways, by which stations on the network are connected to each other. Typically, this architecture, or design, will be one of three concepts:

- *Bus:* Where each station broadcasts its message throughout the network so that all stations hear all messages. Each station must receive and transmit messages in both directions along the cable.
- *Star:* A series of point-to-point links, radiating from a common station, hence a star. In this concept, all transmission passes through and is switched through a central station.
- *Ring:* This method requires each work station to send all messages to its neighbor on one side. Each station must interpret the message, process the ones intended for its own use, and pass along messages intended for others around the ring.

The vehicles or media in LANs, currently being used for transmitting, are twisted pair wires, coaxial cable, or optical fibers. The type of media chosen plays a significant role in the functions of the LAN system due to its transmitting capability. Characteristics of these versions are described below.

Twisted pair has a certain advantage in that telephone wires are already in place. It provides one channel, and distance of the broadcast is determined by modems.

Optical fibers are the least costly method; however, technologically it is currently difficult to tap into the fiber strands.

Coaxial cable is very heavy and must be fed through walls. It can be baseband type, for one way at short distances, or broadband, which divides the cable into many channels, allowing more users to communicate at one time. Coaxial cable can support multiple technologies.

Transmission speed is expressed as bandwidth. Northern Telecom, a leading vendor of telecommunication hardware, describes bandwidth as "the rate at which digitally encoded information can be transmitted."[6] Bandwidth also establishes the speed, type, and quantity of the communication. As stated before, local area networks are in an embryonic stage of development, and these and other options will influence their development. The obvious advantages that LANs offer in allowing the sharing of printers, plotters, facsimile, and large storage devices make them an obvious choice for internal communications. Further, LANs provide the ability to share documents between standalone systems, such as word processors, OCR readers, and microcomputers. As the technology develops and current restrictions are resolved, it is predicted that LANs will provide a means to bring about the long sought, truly automated office.

LAN Vendors

Any listing of vendors of office technologies will quickly become dated; nonetheless, a listing of local area network vendors has significance in that the vendors and products identified represent the first generation of this technology (see Figure 6-7).

Also important to this listing are the product announcements of IBM and AT&T. Both announcements were made in the spring of 1984. The IBM LAN announcement of April, 1984 was long awaited by the industry as other vendors looked to IBM to set the de facto standards. Some parameters announced by IBM were:

- Baseband, all-digital transmission
- Shielded, twisted pair wires and/or fiber optics as the medium
- A star architecture
- Token-passing ring access protocol.

---

[6] *1982 Annual Report,* Northern Telecom Limited, p. 26.

VENDOR	*NETWORK NAME*	*MEDIA*	*P/I**
A.B. Dick	Magna Loop	Baseband	P
Apple Computer, Inc.	AppleBus		P/I
AT&T	ISN	Twisted Pair	P/I
Compucorp	OmegaNet (CSMA/CA)	Baseband	P
Corvus	Omninet	Baseband	I
Datapoint	ARCnet	Baseband	P
		Broadband**	
Digital Equipment Corp.	DECnet	Baseband	P
Hewlett-Packard	AdvanceNet		
IBM	"Data Expressway"	Baseband,	P
	PC/Net	Twisted Pair,	
		and/or Fiber	
		Optics	
Lanier	Business System 5000	Baseband	P
Microsoft	MS-Net		
Mitel	SX-2000 PBX	Twisted Pair	I
Nestor	PLAN	Baseband	I
North Star	NorthNet	Twisted Pair	P
Northern Telecom	SL-1	Twisted Pair	I
Racal-Milgo	Planet	Baseband	I
Rolm	CBX-11	Twisted Pair	I
Syntrex	SynNet	Baseband	P
Sytek	LocalNet	Broadband	I
Ungermann-Bass Inc.	Net One	Baseband	I
Vector Graphics	LINC	Twisted Pair	P
Wang	WangNet	Broadband	P
	FastLan	Broadband	P/I
Xerox/Digital/Intel	Ethernet	Baseband	P/I

* Code: P = Proprietary I = Independent
** Announcements only

Figure 6-7   Local area network vendors.

There were a number of vendors in the marketplace before IBM and AT&T's announcements. However, LANs will become IBM-compatible, as are other devices in office automation due to IBM's major presence in the industry—evidenced by AT&T's announcements. The star topology of the Information Systems Network (ISN), AT&T's local area network, is similar to the IBM system. It will use standard twisted-pair wiring, as well as fiber-optic cable.

We have noted that one of the media for LANs is twisted pair wiring, which is very similar to telephone wiring. Suppliers of PBX systems, such at AT&T and Northern Telecom, have announced local area networking systems to be used through their central telephone equipment to combine both voice and data. The "voice store and forward" technology is one example of the many emerging technologies for the PBX LAN-type systems, and it is anticipated that in the near future the PBX LANs will not be able to handle the increasing traffic. Distributed data and word processing, personal computers, and other office automation devices are in demand to co-exist with voice transmission. New concepts and designs to form a marriage of these technologies, that will accommodate this increased traffic, will undoubtedly be forthcoming from PBX and LAN vendors.[7]

COMMUNICATION SERVICES

The numerous communication services reflect the technologically explosive industry that spawned them; innovative business enterprises are constantly at work creating new services to attract the potential communications user. These services can be valuable when planning for the full use of office automation hardware and software. Identified here is only a partial list of communication services available on personal computers, word processors, or other intelligent work stations with suitable communication capability, which can be used in an office or home environment.

- Dow Jones Services[8]: Dow Jones Services offer full text of the Wall Street Journal at 6 a.m. on the day of publication. Back editions, available to January 3, 1984, can also be accessed by the user of their services. The data base of the newspaper is updated daily. General News and Information services, also provided by Dow Jones, includes: a complete 20-volume encyclopedia, the World Report, and sports and weather information.
- Fidelity Brokerage Services, Inc., Boston, MA[9]: Fidelity Investor's Express (FIE) provides automated securities trading, portfolio analysis, and stock quotations.

[7]Keith Bennetts, "LAN Firm: PBX Makers Still Playing Catch Up," *MIS Week*, 9 May, 1984.

[8]"Wall Street Journal Goes On-Line," *MIS Week*, 30 May, 1984.

[9]"Dial-up for Fast Stock Quotes," *MIS Week*, 30 May, 1984.

- West Publishing Company, St. Paul, MN: WESTLAW® provides a national, full text case law library service. Classified as a computer-assisted legal research system, WESTLAW enables its users to quickly find and research legal precedents.

- Library of Congress, Washington, DC: Provides access to documents, text, and abstract services from books located in the Library of Congress, which is especially attractive to home users.

- PlayNet Inc., Troy, NY: A communications games called "PlayNet" offers users the chance to meet others in an environment similar to a house party. The system is open for interactive [two-way communications] action from 6 p.m. to 7 a.m. seven days a week. The system is available for Commodore, and soon will be for Apple IIs and IBM PCs.[10]

DISCUSSION QUESTIONS

1. Give two examples for the use of communications in word processing.

2. How can compatibility be accomplished between differing systems?

3. Why must all parameters be mirrored in data communications?

4. What is the difference between asynchronous and bisynchronous communications?

5. How do the functions of telecommunications differ from local area networks?

6. What is the current use of twisted pair wires in the office?

7. Why did office automation require the communications capability of LANs?

---

[10]Steve Polilli, "PlayNet Offers National Fun On-Line," *MIS Week,* 11 November, 1984, p. 54.

7

Basics of WP/IP Systems Analysis and Design

Planning is an important phase in any business; planning growth, planning procedures to assure growth, and planning evaluation of results are vital steps that should not be bypassed for the sake of expediency. When the results of a system analysis require the purchase of office automation equipment, these factors take on additional meaning; business must live with equipment decisions, right or wrong, for many years. However, all system evaluations do not necessarily lead to the acquisition of new hardware and software; improvements to procedures can result in increased productivity.

There are no hard and fast rules that must be followed in conducting a study analysis; the rules of common sense should prevail. The major concepts to keep in mind are:

- Determine the business goals of the firm or organization.
- Seek information on how the firm functions.
- Address problems of the particular firm under study.
- Listen to what people have to say and do not assume their answers.

IMPORTANCE OF PREPLANNING

With these preliminary thoughts in mind, the individual or individuals assigned to conducting the study will look for additional team members. Although there is no set number required, it is advisable to keep in mind that when there are too few people, the study effort appears dictatorial; when too many people are involved, decision making becomes difficult. Once the committee is in place, the study team will need to address some basic procedural questions.

Systems Analysis: The study of a task or function to understand it and to determine more efficient methods to accomplish it.

- *Who has authorized the study?* The president or chief operating officer of a company should announce that an office automation study will be conducted. Having top level management authorize and "bless" the activity gives the project a greater chance for success.

- *What is the scope of the study?* Though some guidelines may have been given by management, it is important to have the goals of the study defined so that there will be little opportunity for misunderstanding the scope of the study. Has the problem been defined? Is the entire company to be surveyed, or only a single department? Is the study to cover total office automation, such as reprographics, local area networks, etc., or will the study cover a specific discipline?

- *Who should be involved in the study analysis effort?* All levels of company personnel should be represented on the study team. Upper management, supervisors, and clerical support staff should all be involved. Representatives of marketing, personnel, administration, purchasing and shipping should be on the team. In other words, all phases of an organization should have input, as their varied experiences will add credibility to the effort.

- *What method will be used to conduct the survey?* Numerous options are open to the study team. Their interview process can involve every employee or a selected sampling. The questions can be presented orally or in printed form. The interviews can be conducted by teams or on a one-to-one basis. The study team should choose the method that best suits the particular organization.

Paper Path: Steps involved to create a given report or document.

- *Who should be interviewed?* Just as the study team reflects the overall makeup of the company, so should those being interviewed. For example, the process of seeking information to determine the paper path of a particular report can provide revealing details about the functions and procedures in a company. Interviewing each employee responsible for input and production of that report, as well as those who use the information, will probably reveal duplication of effort or faulty procedures.

There is always the temptation to bypass an annoying individual who you know will take up too much of your valuable time. Of course, there is always the individual who knows what is best for the company because his brother-in-law has a home computer. These types of annoyances must be hurdled; however, a firm plan and schedule will keep the study team on track.

- *Are copies of existing procedures available?* If existing procedures are in written form, the committee members should have copies prior to conducting the interviews. The study team members will be more informed about the principal functions of each department, which will save time during the interview process.

- *How will the study team's findings be recorded?* Once a questionnaire or interview format has been established, the format for compiling the results should be designed. If the organization has word processing capability at its disposal, it is suggested that a records processing file be established for entering data. Lacking this capability, arrangements should be made to have information manually typed in a uniform format for easy analysis. Entering the data as the interviews are completed is strongly advised, as notes tend to get cold and omissions are not noticed until the interviewing cycle has been completed.

Should controversy develop among team members concerning the results of an interview, a copy of the transcript should be returned to the interviewee for his or her approval.

The importance of completing the steps for preplanning cannot be overemphasized; each step in the planning stage has its own value, and shortcutting the process can cause problems when the time for installation arrives.

CONCEPTS OF SYSTEMS DESIGN

What is systems analysis and design? When we make plans for a vacation trip, for example, certain decisions need to be made before we can enjoy the fun. First and foremost, of course, is,

"Where are we going?" Once the destination is decided upon, we must decide what method of transportation to use. The final question is, "What are we going to do when we get there?" Though this analogy may seem simplistic when compared to the complexities of office automation decisions, it is relevant.

Making intelligent decisions about hardware and software to govern office automation is not possible unless a plan has been made for the use and function of those systems. Nor should any plan be made without a clear understanding of the purpose of the company or organization involved. Prior to acquiring any office system it is necessary to ask "Where are we going?" and "What are we going to do when we get there?" The findings of the study team, the analysis of the information, the formation of procedures to implement needed improvements, are sequential steps leading to the creation of a systems design.

Planning and Conducting the Study

In order to proceed in an orderly manner, an outline should be formulated. An outline will serve both as a guideline for the study process and as the basis of the study documentation. Figure 7–1 suggests a sample outline for conducting an office automation and/or word/information processing study analysis. As these steps are critical to the procedure, each phase will be discussed in detail in the order of the outline. To provide a basis of reference for this discussion, the fictional Rancho Engineering Company will be cited. The company's business purpose is the construction of bridges, airport terminals, large sports arenas, etc.

SCOPE OF STUDY

Statement of Purpose

Define in clear terms exactly the reasons for the study; that is, state what information problems and procedures exist. For example, there is a backlog in keyboarding contract agreements in Rancho Engineering's legal department, causing a delay for the field engineering department. This in turn forced the temporary layoff of field employees, which then caused an additional workload for the payroll and personnel departments.

I. SCOPE OF STUDY
   A. Statement of Purpose
   B. Study Objectives
   C. Project Directory
II. ANALYSIS OF EXISTING SYSTEM
   A. Interview Process
   B. Information Requirements
   C. Paper Path Analysis
   D. Existing Hardware and Software
III. STATEMENT OF EXISTING SYSTEM
   A. Statement of Information Requirements
   B. Analysis of Existing Procedures
IV. PROPOSED SYSTEM DESIGN
   A. Recommended Procedural Solutions
   B. Recommended Hardware and Software Solutions
V. SUMMARY OF FINDINGS
   A. Report Summary
   B. Prioritizing Recommendations
APPENDIX
   A. Study Team Directory
   B. Glossary of Terms

Figure 7-1 Study outline.

To add to the domino effect, the personnel department had difficulty locating field personnel because current lists were not available. The president or CEO of Rancho Engineering should issue a statement identifying the scope of the study analysis and requesting the full cooperation of the entire company. Stating the problem and the fact that the company is willing to seek solutions encourages a spirit of cooperation which will enhance the chances for success of the project.

Study Objectives

Exactly what is to be achieved by the study should be stated. The direction given to the team by management should be restated here. Such a statement, reflecting Rancho Engineering's conditions, sets forth the objectives:

1. To determine the source, input, and processing of information necessary to achieve the business goals of the company.

2. To propose policies and procedures to ensure the efficient processing of information.

3. To recommend, if necessary, hardware and software acquisitions to implement the proposed policies and procedures.

Project Directory

The purpose of the project directory is to provide a list of all persons and areas of the company involved in the study: study team members and employees interviewed. The directory should include the employee's name, title, department location, and telephone number.

ANALYSIS OF EXISTING SYSTEM

Interview Process

The people involved in the actual production of a report or task have the most knowledge about its requirements. For example, the personnel clerk at Rancho Engineering responsible for the initial interviews with prospective employees is fully aware of the information requirements of the employment application. This employee would be aware of any information omitted from the form which required additional contact with the applicant once he or she was hired. Simply interviewing the manager of the personnel department would probably not reveal this omission of information. Involving management and support personnel allows a more complete picture of procedures to be developed. In this manner, each level of personnel has the opportunity to state the procedure or problem, as they view it.

Information Requirements

The major focus of the interview process is to determine the business purpose and the information requirements of the departments under study. It is important to determine the function that employees fulfill in providing and processing the required information. To examine the examples further, is Rancho Engineering's legal department experiencing a backlog because the necessary information does not reach them in a timely manner? Is the engineering department having to cut back on personnel because the contracts are not approved quickly enough to be forwarded to the clients for signature? Or could the difficulty be found in the word processing procedures for storing boilerplate material?

Paper Path Analysis

Following the paper path of a report assists the analyst in understanding the life cycle of information. To assist in the analyzing process, it is advisable for each project under study to be diagrammed or flow-charted to assist in the identification of information sources and destinations. For example, before Rancho Engineering's data processing department can produce a quarterly budget status report, several departments must provide data input (see Figure 7–2). The personnel department must report all new hires, promotions, and dismissals to the payroll department. If the deadlines are not met by the personnel department, the payroll and employee status information will be incomplete. In turn, the quarterly budget analysis versus actual figures will be inaccurate or delayed. By flow-charting the path of information requirement for the

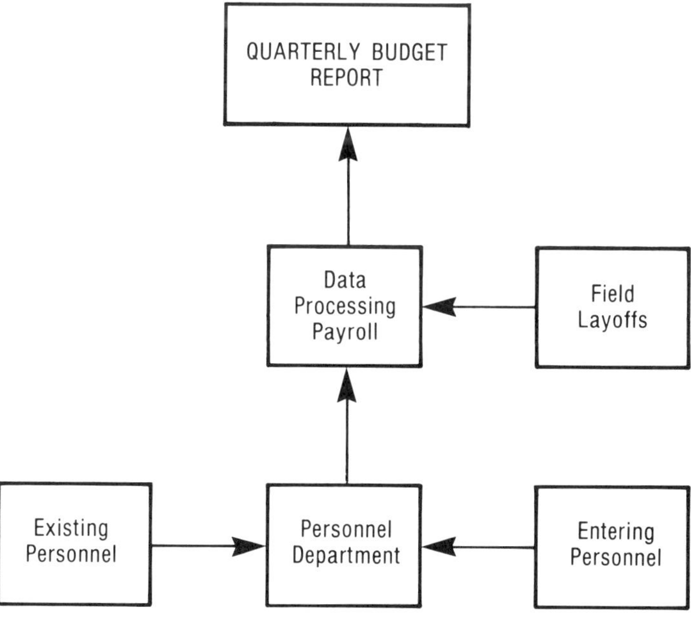

Figure 7-2   Paper path flow chart.

quarterly report, the study team will have a better understanding of departmental requirements.

Existing Hardware and Software

When studies are conducted in firms where word processing, data processing, or other identifiable office automation systems exist, an inventory of all hardware and software should be completed. Included in the inventory should be the vendor name and model, and the version of software currently being used. In addition, all peripheral devices and software should be listed, such as communication features, electronic mail, voice store and forward, facsimile, etc. Where possible, vendor documentation of the purpose and capability of all devices should be in the study team's possession. It is not unusual to find that software functions are underutilized or not used at all.

In addition to the hardware and software inventory, a separate list should be prepared of word processing operator personnel citing their training and experience level. This list will serve two purposes: 1) a tool to identify personnel for assistance in system implementation and 2) assist in identifying future training requirements of operator personnel.

STATEMENT OF EXISTING SYSTEM

Information Requirements

Once the interview and fact-finding phase has been completed, the study team members should compile the data in an orderly format by categories as previously discussed.

Analysis of Existing Procedures

In addition to the flow charts describing the path of information, a set of parameters to assist in evaluating current procedures should be established. The members of the study team, in analyzing their information, will probably find duplication of effort, lack of proper information, and overlapping responsibilities. For example, information is often compiled in an incorrect format and has to be manually reformatted before it can be used. It is common to find two or more departments creating the same information base, yet only extracting a portion for their own use.

In analyzing machine processing functions, the team will need to have a good comprehension of the installed equipment, as well as the de facto standards of the industry. For example, Rancho Engineering's personnel department is responsible for the production of a salary report sorted by department. To accomplish this task, the information processing equipment being used should have a records processing or list processing capability. If this report is to be combined with other departmental reports, the format, size and printing capability should be standardized to alleviate last minute reproduction of documents.

PROPOSED SYSTEM DESIGN

Recommended Procedural Solutions

The study team should state in their report the procedures presently being followed and identify procedures that require change. These procedures should be identified, followed by the recommendation for change, noting the benefits to be achieved, as shown in Figure 7–3.

Problem Identification	The word processing facility in Rancho Engineering's legal department is experiencing a two-week backlog in contract production even though a night shift has been employed
Procedure	The five attorneys in the legal department present their work in handwritten form or by dictation. The majority of the material is repetitive and the attorneys refer the word processing staff to previous documents for these "boilerplate" sections. As the operators seldom have the diskette at hand where the designated document resides, they usually retype the material.
Problem Solution	The three word-processing machines installed in the legal department are adequate to handle the workload of the five attorneys. The creation of basic document diskettes for each operator will greatly increase productivity. These documents should be recorded by paragraph number, and a printout of these standard paragraphs given to each attorney. Only the information unique to the individual contact will be dictated or handwritten. Standard document fill-in forms should be created so that the attorneys need only write the paragraph numbers in the proper sequential order when composing a document.
Benefits to Be Derived	By using the paragraph assembly feature of the word processing equipment, the operators should experience a marked increase in productivity. Further, the night shift of operators will not be required. This type of recording procedure should be employed company-wide for the creation of standard documents.

Figure 7-3 Procedural Solutions.

Recommended Hardware and Software Solutions

There will be occasions when only hardware or software changes can provide a solution to information processing problems. An example of this type of solution can be seen in Figure 7-4.

SUMMARY OF FINDINGS

Report Summary

The report summary should pull together the analysis of the interviews and the study team's recommendations. The solutions to identified problems should be clearly stated in the report summary. Wherever possible, costs of implementing the recommendations should be included. At this stage of the systems development, costs of recommended hardware and software would have to be approximated. Costs and savings as a result of procedural recommendations can be more difficult to define; however, they should be included.

The physical report should be produced as a formal document and its findings presented orally to the level of management authorizing the study analysis.

Problem Identification	The word processing software being used in the personnel department does not provide an automatic merge from a file of records. The department is required to maintain alphabetized employee lists for frequent mailings. The operators manually alphabetize several lists for reports and mailings.
Procedure	The personnel department sends out standard response letters to inquiries for employment. Alphabetized lists are maintained of these employee prospects as well as lists of current employees, insurance program participants, and the employee telephone directory.
Problem Solution	Acquire the software to provide auto merge and sorting capability. Acquire 64K of additional memory to handle the increased function.
Benefits to Be Derived	Merged letters to prospective employees and the required alphabetized list can be accomplished from a single file. The increased software function can also be utilized to produce the telephone directory, maintain the insurance program lists, and produce labels in zip code order for the company newsletter, all from a single file.

Figure 7-4   Recommended hardware and software solutions.

PRIORITIZING RECOMMENDATIONS

The report should also include a prioritized calendar for implementation of the recommended information processing solutions.

INTEGRATION OF OFFICE AUTOMATION (OA) PERIPHERALS

Peripheral Devices: Those technologies where intelligent machines support the processing of information.

Throughout the interview process, a study team will be confronted with opportunities to incorporate office automation functions other than those provided by dedicated word processors and microcomputers. Solutions to some of Rancho Engineering's problems could have been found in what are known as peripheral devices. For example, perhaps Rancho Engineering could resolve the delay in client contract approval by installing a facsimile machine to telecommunicate the completed contract document directly to the client. Or in the case of the backlog in printing of contracts, Rancho Engineering could choose to install a laser printer that could be used company-wide through the communications capability of the company's word processors. In today's world of office automation technologies, many information processing solutions are available, some of which are discussed here.

Communicating Peripheral Devices

As we learned in Chapter 6, local area network (LAN) systems are designed to allow information processing terminals to share other OA devices. These devices can be activated from the keyboard via telecommunications or through hookup with a LAN system. These peripheral information processing systems provide additional dimension to office automation and, in many instances, they provide unique functions not found in word or data processors. However, these devices should also be judged by de facto standards of the particular industry. How these peripherals can be integrated into office functions is discussed here.

Intelligent Printers

These high-volume quality printers have the communications capability to send or receive documents in multi-font styles. They are also standard printing devices for LAN systems, thus accommodating high volume requirements; however, the cost has generally discouraged their use by small organizations. There are primarily two technologies represented in intelligent printers.

Ink-Jet Printers

Printing speeds now range to 92 cps (characters per second) as compared to 60 cps on impact, daisywheel printers. Scaled down table-top versions are now offered for lower volume use (see Figure 7–5, Exxon 965 desktop ink-jet printer).

Laser Printers

The Xerox 5700 laser printer is used for communications, as well as in-house volume printing. Many vendors offer laser

Figure 7-5　Exxon office systems' 965 ink-jet printer. (*Courtesy Exxon Office Systems Company.*)

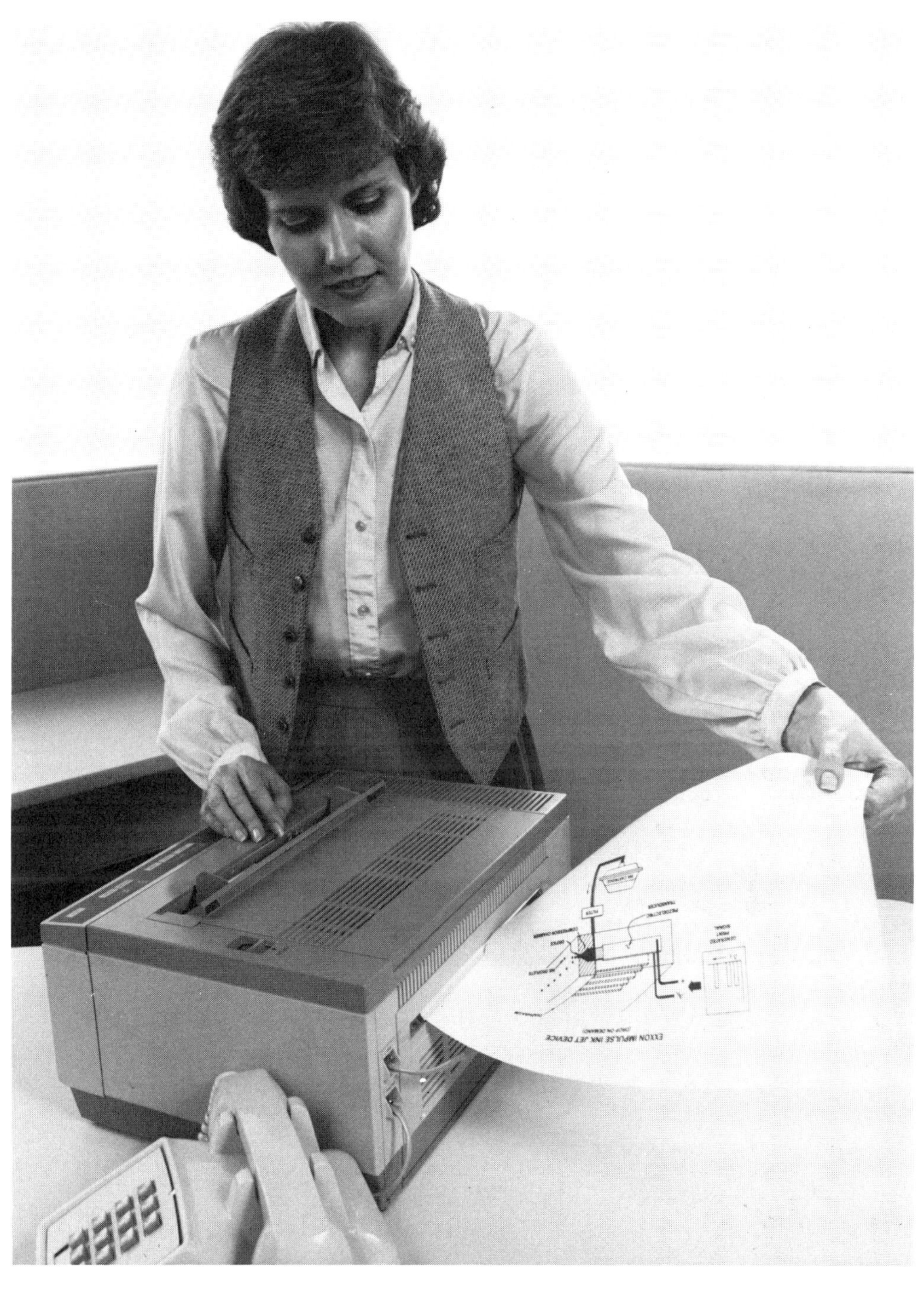

Figure 7-6 Exxon Office Qwip 2310.® (*Courtesy Exxon Office Systems Company.*)

technology with dedicated word processing systems. Both the large and small laser printers are being used on LAN systems.

Plotters

Plotters are used in engineering environments to display numerical input graphically. Plotters differ from printers in that they use color and shadings of print in the output.

Facsimile

This technology was introduced in the early 1970s. Several generic names for the technology have resulted from well-accepted vendor products, such as *telecopier,* a trademark of Xerox Corporation. Exxon Office Systems' Qwip (see Figure 7–6) also produced a generic term. The latest model of Exxon's Qwip, 2210, is a companion satellite to the company's full-featured model 2310 Qwip. The Panafax MV-3000 (see Figure 7–7) facsimile can receive information directly from a word processor, personal computer, or computer terminal. The accompanying X.25 packet-switched option has the ability to transmit material in a store-and-forward mode or on a broadcast basis.

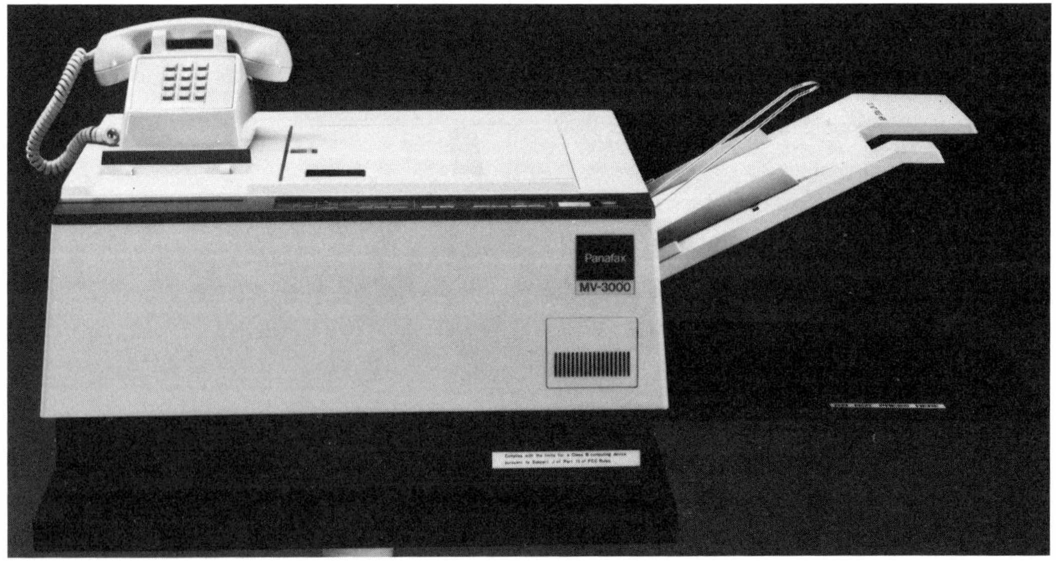

Figure 7-7   Panafax MV-3000. (*Courtesy Panafax Corporation.*)

Figure 7-8   CompuScan AlphaWord® Series 80 PageReader. (*Courtesy CompuScan Corporation.*)

Phototypesetters

Communicating to phototypesetters from word processors became commonplace in the early 1980s. These devices have become extremely sophisticated components in office automation installations. They are CRT-oriented and microprocessor-based, allowing them to be upgraded by increasing memory and adding improved software.

Optical Character Readers (OCR)

Scanning devices have also experienced a giant technology leap in the 1980s. In addition to the traditional function of scanning typewritten pages for word processing input, they have become sophisticated communicators. The CompuScan AlphaWord PageReader (see Figure 7–8) provides communication capability to word and data processors, phototypesetters, TWX, Telex, and intelligent terminals. Laser technology has also been applied to OCR devices and is used mainly for high speed data entry.

Electronic Mail (EM)

Defined as a form of electronic communication, the concept can be fulfilled through a number of devices. Various technologies are used for distribution of electronic mail such as facsimile, telex, TWX, Teletext, interpersonal mail services (IPMS), and word processors. Though the technology is currently void of standards, the Consultative Committee on International Telephony and Telegraphy have approved international electronic mail standards for data communications.

Media Conversion Options

OCR technology also plays a major role in media conversion technology. Kurzweil Computer Products, Inc. combines OCR

Figure 7-9   Kurzweil Altertext OCR Scanner. (*Courtesy Kurzweil Computer Products.*)

technology with computer software in their Altertext system to scan documents and output them to any word or data processing format (see Figure 7–9). The operator can scan several pages of a document to determine if any characters are unreadable. If this occurs, the operator can instruct the system to recognize the foreign character the next time it occurs and replace it with the proper one. Conversely, the operator can instruct the system to ignore or replace characters. The Kurzweil system has been designed with an Ethernet LAN connection.

Communicating through a converter system, often referred to as a "black box," which changes coding formats from one system to another, provides a compatibility for differing word processing systems, as shown in the communication session 4 of the previous chapter.

Back-Up Energy Sources

Disk Crashes: Unreadable data.

As a power failure can cause disk crashes and loss of information, many word processing installations are investing in power protection devices. These plug-in regulators are available to protect against voltage fluctuation or to protect against power outages of two to four hours duration.

MAKING VENDOR DECISIONS

If a comprehensive system analysis study has been completed and documented, making vendor decisions can be a pleasurable experience. The recognized de facto standards established for the word/information processing industry and the study team's recommendations will greatly assist the task of making hardware and software decisions. There is a great temptation on the part of organizations to venture into vendor's demonstration rooms; vendors are always happy to see you and show their latest technology. However, these demonstrations take a great deal of time, and after four or five such visits, the functions and keyboard procedures become blurred in the viewer's mind. Whether an organization is installing OA devices for the first time or looking for upgrading of capability, using the Request for Proposal method is the most professional way to interview vendors and schedule demonstrations.

Request for Proposal (RFP)

An RFP is a standard method of requesting technical information about a vendor's equipment, services, and costs. The RFP outlines the exact function and physical features desired by the company. If an organization has budget limitations, that information should also be included along with a closing date for accepting proposals.

Sending an RFP helps to alleviate the crush of vendor sales representatives pressing for appointments and allows the equipment task committee to contact vendors in an orderly and controlled manner. When the RFP deadline has been reached, the proposals are viewed and decisions narrowed down to no more than four prospective vendors. This is the appropriate time to make contact with vendors and request an appointment time for equipment demonstrations. Most demonstrations will require a period of two to three hours so that thorough explanations and a "hands-on" session by the operator(s) can be accomplished. The major items to be included in an RFP are shown in Figure 7–10.

Selecting a vendor requires investigation into areas other than the electronic function of the equipment. The study team will want to inquire into the technical support provided by vendors under consideration.

- Secure from the vendors a list of firms who are in a similar industry and who use the model of equipment being considered.

- Ask the firms using the equipment about response time of service personnel when the systems are down.

- Request a copy of the vendor's most recent annual report. If a company has been losing money for several years in their word processing division, chances are they will not be in business very long.

Ergonomic Considerations

The importance of user comfort with VDTs is expressed by the fact that the subject matter is discussed in three different chapters of this textbook; ergonomics and VDTs are discussed here

---

REQUEST FOR PROPOSAL (RFP)*

The six basic areas to be addressed in an RFP are as follows:

1) **System Architecture**
   - Operating system(s)
   - Type of processor
   - Floppy/hard disk storage capacities
   - Memory size
   - Number of terminals supported
   - Printers supported
   - Peripherals supported

2) **Software**
   - Basic word processing
   - Math functions
   - File processing
   - Sort Capacity
   - Graphics
   - Spelling
   - Other software availability

3) **Communications Parameters**
   - Protocols supported
   - Networks available
   - Peripherals available

4) **Costs**
   - Purchase, lease and rental figures of hardware and software
   - Shipping and installation
   - Maintenance
   - Taxes and tax credits

5) **Training**
   - Costs
   - Basic training plan
   - Future training plan
   - Materials available
   - Personnel available
   - What training comes with the system, what additional training is available
   - Upgrading

6) **References**
   - Names, addresses and telephone numbers of like users

Figure 7-10   Request for proposal.

as they relate to vendor equipment decisions. It is important to solicit the operator's opinion of a system. He or she should insist on having the opportunity to try the keyboard and work with the software functions. If the screen resolution is poor or the tilting adjustments do not allow for operator comfort, this is the time to discover such ergonomic problems. It is also a good time to be aware if printers require acoustical hoods to subdue excessive printer noise.

DISCUSSION QUESTIONS

1. Who should be involved in a systems design study? Who should be interviewed?
2. What is the purpose of an office automation plan?
3. Who should announce plans for an OA study?
4. What is the major focus of the interview process?
5. Describe the paper path analysis.
6. If you are currently training on word/information processing equipment, what procedure(s) would you suggest to solve Rancho Engineering's problem in the legal department (see Figure 7–3)?
7. How can communicating peripherals assist in information processing?
8. Why is OCR equipment important to media conversion?
9. What is the purpose of the RFP?

8

Implementing Information Processing Systems

Once the vendor decision has been made and delivery dates have been established, it is time to prepare an implementation plan.[1] No matter how well the previous planning stages have proceeded, the time period leading up to equipment installation holds many frustrating experiences for the organization that fails to plan for installation day.

PRE-INSTALLATION

Calendar for Implementation

Of course, the expected delivery date marks the point of implementation; however, a number of events should be planned and coordinated prior to that date, such as training, user orientation, procedures manuals for users and word processing personnel, vendor coordination for installation, and building preparation. Though delivery schedules may vary from vendor to vendor, two months can normally be expected between the contract signing and the delivery dates. This interim period can be put to good advantage by planning the implementation calendar and following through with the suggestions in this chapter.

Introducing the System

Conducting a systems analysis study in any company gives rise to concerns among employees about how their jobs will be affected once the new system is in place. This is a natural reaction, as office automation can bring changes in job descriptions,

---

[1]Mary E. Locke and Paula Calise, "Taking Control of Automation," *Management World,* October 1983, p. 20.

work environments, and salaries. Anxieties about employee layoffs also intrude when a company is installing OA equipment for the first time. The new system should be explained to all levels of personnel involved as soon as the vendor decision has been made. This may even require a company-wide meeting or less formal, departmental level meetings if the acquisition is of such magnitude. By discussing the benefits of the new system and bringing everyone up to date regarding delivery schedules, training plans, etc., all of the employees can share in the implementation plans.

Beta Testing

Depending upon the vendor's rental policies, securing a rental version of the system to be acquired can be of great assistance in operator training, establishing and testing procedures, and determining space and furniture requirements. If renting a version of the equipment on order is not possible, there are a number of outside services available from word/information processing service bureaus and training centers. Beta testing should not be construed as "testing" in the sense of decision-making; however, it does give an organization the opportunity to determine whether the system can perform as promised.

Managerial Orientation

One of the greatest causes of failure of office automation installations occurs when one or more levels of management refuse to use the system because they "like the old manual method better." Social scientists suggest that people are comfortable with the "old ways," and sometimes feel threatened by new technology. This can be overcome with proper orientation to allow the user to feel in control of the system, rather than the system having control over the user.

Applications Design

An effective way to introduce users to any system is to place one of their applications on the system. As you will recall in our fictitious company, Rancho Engineering, the personnel department was responsible for a number of reports. One of the manager's major reports provided the Data Processing Department with salary information of new hires and promotions. Additional input was supplied by the Field Engineering department relative to temporary layoffs. As this project was one of the smaller files applications addressed by the study team, it could be designed and input into the system quickly, thus making it available during training seminars. Most vendors are willing to allow the customer to accomplish this size task, if equipment is available, on a beta test arrangement.

The beta testing of applications is a good practice for several reasons. You will recall that in Chapter 3 we learned that documents could be produced in a variety of ways, depending upon the de facto standards present in the software and hardware of the system. However, choosing the correct function is the key to productive word processing; beta testing helps accomplish this goal.

Let's look at Application 1 of the sample exercises in Chapter 3, dealing with creation of engineering specifications. The procedure suggested in the chapter was to use the paragraph assembly function. As you recall, this de facto standard allows paragraphs to be stored separately with an identifying name or number for easy recall. Our sample company, Rancho Engineering, may find that since so much of the document is "boilerplate" material, the best application of the de facto standards would be to use the variable merge function instead of merging a file with text. Using variable merge would require duplicating or using a "GET" function, depending upon the vendor, and creating a list of variables for automatic merge. Beta testing procedure is a vital part of installing a system.

Operator Training

Training of operators prior to installation will help ensure the rapid adoption and integration of information processing equipment and procedures. It would be impossible to train a large staff in such a short period of time; however, it is conceivable that the supervisor and lead operator could be trained in a beta test situation. Early training will also be of value when making application design decisions.

User Training

Once procedures for utilizing the new office automation services have been established, training for users should begin. Training in this context encompasses such user concerns as how to submit work to be keyboarded and processed, how the resident de facto standards provide options and strengths to produce work, and the procedures for final editing and storage of documents.

Some manufacturers and third party vendors are offering interactive video training systems for users of microcomputers. Interaction with the equipment is a very effective training method. With this method, special programs are used which explain a topic, and present questions on the screen which must be answered correctly before proceeding to the next topic.

These training or briefing sessions should also address application design questions and the plans for feedback from users, discussed further under "Monitoring the System" in this chapter.

Integration of Installed Systems

Anyone who has ever had experience with installing an office automation facility, whether word processing or data processing, knows that "everything that can go wrong will go wrong"—the all-too-familiar "Murphy's Law." This is especially true when dealing with dissimilar or incompatible technologies, namely electrical, cooling, and telephone systems. Some of these frustrations can be avoided by requesting a copy of the technical specifications of the equipment from the vendor. The following items should be examined and coordinated with the persons responsible for the building facility.

- Power requirements for work stations, printers, and controllers.
- Humidity and temperature ranges.
- Dimensions and weight of equipment.
- Communication specifications for modems (see list in Chapter 6).

- Cabling requirements to direct connection devices and networking systems.

Telephone communication plans should be discussed with the appropriate local telephone company, or in certain cases, AT&T, at the earliest possible opportunity. If the company includes a data processing department, the DP manager can be of great assistance in unraveling the telephone connection mysteries, as most of them have been involved in the same pre-installation communications phase. Of course, if data processing capability is present in a firm, a member representing that department should have been on the study team.

Ergonomics and Productivity

No one wants to work in an office that is hot in the summer and cold in the winter, so noisy they can't carry on a telephone conversation, or where poor lighting and inadequate furniture lead to eyestrain and backaches. In a survey of productivity involving an energy-saving cutback in candlepower at the Social Security Administration in the 1970s, it was revealed that productivity decreased 28% when the candlepower was reduced from 100c to 50c; when the candlepower was restored to 100c, productivity climbed back to its original level.[2] These problems should be the concern not only of people operating computer-oriented equipment, but also of the study team during the pre-installation phase.

As discussed in an earlier chapter, the elimination or prevention of glare is of great importance in the use of CRT stations. A CRT screen should be placed in the planned work area prior to installation to determine the existence of poor lighting and glare conditions.

Excessive noise can also be anti-productive. If an OA system with noisy printers was chosen, acoustical hoods that reduce impact printing noises should be purchased. The study of office planning is a recognized discipline established for the professional planning of work areas and office environment.

---

[2]"Improving the Quality of Light . . . and Work Performance," *Office Administration and Automation*, May 1984, p. 39–40.

Several titles related to office planning and ergonomics are listed in the Bibliography.

POST-INSTALLATION

When news is received that the new OA equipment is sitting on the receiving department's dock, the post-installation period begins. Expectations have been running high, many applications for the system have been identified, and perhaps some annoyance over the delay of installation has been experienced. After all the careful planning by the study team, it seems impossible that anything could go wrong at this stage; however, "Murphy's Law" applies to the post-installation phase, too. Some appropriate suggestions to assure that the final phase can avoid the disenchantment of the prospective users are discussed in this section.

Vendor Participation

During the period of equipment selection, vendor attention runs high. However, the reality of the salesperson's world is making sales and quotas; when installation time arrives, technical vendor support personnel should be present. Depending upon the vendor(s), this personnel could be represented by marketing service representatives who provide technical assistance, or by service engineers who assist in the setting up and testing of the equipment. Many vendors do not provide any set-up assistance at all; instructions for set-up and testing arrive with the equipment. The vendor's policies for installation should be determined by the study team prior to delivery, thus allowing time to learn how the set-up is to be accomplished.

Phasing in Applications

Consideration should be given to a phase-in plan, either on a departmental level or project level. For example, large data base projects require considerable keyboarding time; standard paragraph selection projects, that utilize previously stored material, can be accomplished in a short period of time. The priority schedule prepared during the study phase is a valuable tool during this period. Operator expertise and training schedules can also dictate application priorities.

Educating New Staff and Users

Training new word/information processing operators is an ongoing task for any organization, and deserves some planning time. Vendors may offer to train one or two operators per station; however, most vendors have limits on training. Regardless of the size of an organization, having in-house courses for new operators and for upgrading operator skills is advisable.

New user personnel need to be considered in the training plan, too. Because of the acceptance of office automation today, there is the possibility that new employees will have already been accustomed to using the particular type of equipment installed. However, it will still be necessary to inform new users about particular procedures and practices of their new company.

Monitoring the System

Considering the investment in time and money when office automation equipment has been installed, the monitoring of the system for user satisfaction and achievement of the system design goals is mandatory. This can be accomplished by periodic review or on a project-by-project basis. By providing an invitation to users to give feedback on a day-to-day basis, there is little opportunity for discontent to develop. This type of communication and monitoring plan helps to keep the word/information processing effort at its peak of proficiency and productivity.

INFORMATION SECURITY

In June of 1984, a computer bank containing credit information on some nine million individuals was invaded by outside sources through a telecommunications intrusion. During the previous year, news headlines disclosed that a group of teenagers with access to microcomputers, through a random selection of passwords, used telecommunications to invade computer data banks of several large corporations. The American Bar Association (ABA) released the results of a study on computer crime in which some 150 companies indicated that computer crimes have created losses averaging from $2 million to $10 million.[3] The ABA further revealed that of the 1,000 companies involved in the study, 40 percent had evidence of losses due to computer crimes, such as "unauthorized use of business computers for personal use, theft of software, theft of tangible or intangible assets through use of a computer, theft of hardware, and destruction or alteration of data stored in a computer."[4]

Security of computer data bases has become one of the nation's major concerns, and because of this, some 25 states have passed computer crime legislation. The problem has also been addressed by the United States Congress. In the 98th Congress, 2d session of the House of Representatives, H.R. 5616 "Counterfeit Access Device and Computer Fraud and Abuse Act of 1984," was introduced. The act would find persons guilty of fraud and assign penalties if anyone

> (1) knowingly accesses a computer without authorization or, having accessed a computer with authorization, uses the opportunity such access provides for purposes to which such authorization does not extend, with the intent to execute a scheme to defraud ... obtains anything of value (other than the computer) aggregating $5,000 or more during any one year period;

> (2) knowingly accesses a computer without authorization or, having accessed a computer with authorization, uses the opportunity such access provides for purposes to which such authorization does not extend, and by means of one or more instances of such conduct knowingly uses, modifies, or discloses information in, or prevents authorized use of, such computer, if—

[3]Dan Tregoboff, "ABA Says CPU Crime Rampant," *MIS Week*, 20 June, 1984, p. 6.
[4]Ibid.

(A) the offense affects interstate or foreign commerce and the offender thereby obtains anything of value or creates a loss to another of a value aggregating $5,000 or more during any one year period, or

(B) such computer is operated for or on behalf of the United States Government and the prohibited conduct affects such operation.

The proposed bill goes on to list penalties and fines for persons found guilty under the act. This legislative action has been well received in light of the extreme abuses of computer access currently taking place in the United States.

Computer Ethics

Though most word/information systems are not in an "on-line" mode that can be accessed by outsiders, opportunities do exist for internal destruction of valuable information. Disgruntled or improperly trained employees can be a threat to stored information. The easy access to word/information processing terminals and printers finds employees using the equipment's capabilities with much the same attitude as when making personal calls from the telephones on their desks. Though the cost of a printout may be small, the theft in time is significant. Invading data bases and files that have been designated as proprietary information is ethically improper; utilizing information processing equipment for personal reasons falls into the same classification as using another's automobile without permission.

Proprietary Information: Exclusive property belonging to the owner of information.

Media Storage

External media; e.g., floppy disks or diskettes, need to be protected against the elements as well as against theft. Diskettes should be properly stored in protective devices, as they are subject to damage from heat, dirt, and water. Desktop storage is available for disks that are used daily; however, for non-operating periods, all diskettes should be stored in fire- and water-proofed cabinets.

DISCUSSION QUESTIONS

1. What steps should be included in an implementation plan?
2. What is meant by beta testing?
3. Why should managers be involved in OA installation plans?
4. Describe how the electrical and air-conditioning systems can have an impact on office automation.
5. How can productivity be affected by ergonomics?
6. What is the reason for an applications phase-in plan?
7. In your opinion, what steps can be taken to prevent computer crime?
8. How can magnetic media be protected from damage?

9

Career Opportunities in Information Processing

In Chapter 1, we discussed the "Information Age" and the changes brought about by the United State's economy moving away from an industrial society. Many businesses now find that one of their most important assets is information. This change in direction for business has also brought changes in the type of jobs people hold. Today, over 55 percent of the work force in the U.S. is employed in white-collar jobs. To put it another way, over half of the work force is employed in office-oriented jobs.

Office automation technologies have spawned the information age and as a result, OA has made significant changes in the office and in the way we work. New technologies have created jobs that were nonexistent 10 years ago, and in many cases, just five years ago. These new information-oriented positions will be available only to those applicants who have a working knowledge of office functions and technologies. Further, the continuing changes in technology will require constant additional education on the part of these job holders, as forecasts of office automation consultants show that new products and functions will probably develop at a more rapid pace that in the 1970s. Keeping up with technology will be a mandatory requirement for those who expect to succeed in the office automation disciplines.

OPPORTUNITIES IN BUSINESS

The office environment has experienced a great change during the past 10 to 15 years. As the technologies of office automation move closer to the worker's desk in the form of tools for increased productivity, management strategies and procedures to manage information processing have also been the target of change. For example, when word processing equipment was first introduced, secretarial support functions were given two classifications: administrative tasks and keyboarding tasks. Administrative tasks such as dealing with mail, filing, and phones were performed by secretaries and keyboarding tasks were performed in centers where word processing operators were separated from the normal social environment. This concept prevailed for a period of time until dissatisfaction developed among operators of the equipment, as well as among managers served by them.

Management countered with the "cluster" concept where keyboarding and administrative secretaries worked together to provide a variety of functions required for office support. After experimenting with the cluster, word processing power has finally been moved to the secretary's desk, where the equipment is used to provide total administrative and secretarial support. Though some major corporations still use centers, the center concept is no longer dominant in providing word/information processing support. The integrated processing provided by mini and mainframe computers has also brought about necessary changes in management style and organization.

This overall structure evolution has had a positive effect, in that a new structure of administrative management has developed to oversee the integration of office automation technologies. Though career ladders differ from one company to another, careers in information processing offer challenging and exciting opportunities.

The Association of Information Systems Professionals (AISP), in their annual poll of industry salaries, identifies the following career ladder categories for word/information processing professionals:

WP Trainee	WP Trainer
WP Operator	Proofreader
WP Specialist I	WP Supervisor
WP Specialist II/Assistant Supervisor	WP Manager
	Staff/Systems Analyst
Phototypesetting Specialist	Information Manager

Current salary levels for the United States and Canada can be obtained from the organization (see section on professional organizations in this chapter).

The pathways in information processing careers are now traveled by both data processing and word processing aspirants, as well as representatives of the many other office automation disciplines discussed in this text.

Systems Analyst

This position requires a sound knowledge of how an office functions, as well as the interrelated functions in business. The systems analyst must have a complete understanding of the concepts of office automation technologies as discussed in Chapter 7. Though this is a technically oriented position, it is important that the individual have a knowledge of interpersonal skills to understand the impact of administrative decisions. The systems analyst will assist in the dissemination of information by identifying the appropriate procedures and equipment functions.

Supervisory Positions

Supervisory positions require a thorough knowledge of how a company functions, as well as a thorough understanding of the concepts of word/information processing. Because of these technical demands, many supervisors of word/information processing personnel were former operators. Any supervisory position requires a basic understanding of personnel management, and the skills involved are as applicable to office automation personnel as in any other discipline.

Administrative Management

Increasingly, the management step on this career ladder will require a college degree, plus experience in office automation disciplines. Knowledge of data processing, word processing, communications, and the many OA technologies will be beneficial in achieving this position. In addition, knowledge of the role of traditional business functions, such as marketing, accounting, and administration will be necessary.

Personnel Opportunities

During this period of rapid technology development, personnel offices are experiencing a knowledge gap. When asked to fill the position of a word processing operator of a specific vendor origin, knowledge of records processing, glossary, and document assembly, the personnel staff is often at a loss. The representatives in personnel departments have tended to fill these positions by interviewing secretaries who may never have seen word processing equipment. Generally this results in a significant underutilization of the equipment's capabilities, unless an adequate training period is set aside.

Frequently, experienced operators of a different brand of equipment are hired with the belief that a word processor is a word processor. Lacking standardization, the operators in this situation can find themselves at a substantial disadvantage while making the transition. Whether the operator does or does not understand the concepts of word processing is seldom discussed. Persons who are seeking a career in the personnel field, who have an understanding of office automation technologies, should find exciting opportunities in this information age.

Careers in Education

Becoming a teacher of office automation technologies requires a comprehensive knowledge of the industry, plus enthusiasm for keeping abreast of the rapid changes in office technologies, in addition to the prerequisite of a teaching degree. This field should be an exciting and challenging opportunity, as information processing literacy will be in great demand for decades to come. Teachers will find that attending seminars, reading industry literature, and becoming involved in information processing organizations will make this task easier.

In 1984, the Source Telecomputing Corporation introduced a nationwide agreement with the National Computer Training Institute (NCTI) to participate in a nationwide program to train teachers in the use of personal computers. NCTI expected to enroll some 25,000 teachers in the program the first year. IBM Corporation became involved in the project by loaning 15 PC Juniors to each of the 49 school campuses involved.

Vendor Equipment Sales

Most manufacturers of office automation hardware and software require that successful applicants must have a college degree, but there is little uniformity in the required discipline. As always, though, working in sales requires an outgoing personality and attention to detail. Sales positions also require that a person be a self-starter and have a certain degree of self-discipline. Understanding office automation technologies and how they are integrated is basic to the OA salesperson.

ENTREPRENEURIAL OPPORTUNITIES

Opportunities abound for service-oriented businesses in the office automation disciplines. Service bureaus were the first type of business to appear in support of the word processing industry. The support areas of communications, OA consulting, word-processing temporary help services, and information-processing product and hardware sales, all offer opportunities for the individual who has the desire to be self-employed. Even the home building trade now offers microcomputers in newly built houses to entice buyers; supplying the hardware, software and computer expertise for this industry will most likely be in demand in the near future.

EMERGING TECHNOLOGIES

Few professionals in the word and information processing field can honestly state that they are knowledgeable about all the state-of-the-art concepts and technologies impacting office automation today. Office automation is an extremely fertile field for any technology that can improve the manner in which information is processed and distributed. What is important to the aspiring professional in the related fields of office automation is that he or she continue a plan of self-education. Viewed here are a few emerging technologies that are finding acceptance in office automation. Perhaps these technologies will become part of de facto standards for information processing in the office automation effort.

Videotex

Though business and industry are taking a hard look at videotex, it was originally targeted for home use. This technology provides for the delivery of information from computer data bases telecommunicated over telephone or cable lines. A practical business application in the oil industry, for example, would be to receive the complete text of a bill pending in Congress that would affect oil or gas pricing. In the home, for instance, forecasters see it used for shopping, banking and library document retrieval. In either case, the information could be received directly on a word processor, computer or microcomputer, and stored on magnetic media for current viewing or future use. To further the prospects of this technology, IBM, CBS, Inc. and Sears Roebuck have announced a joint venture to "develop a commercial videotex service for users of personal and home computers."[1]

Voice Recognition Processing

Engineers have been developing and testing voice processing for a good many years, for it has been fraught with technical hurdles. The primary target for this function, which allows speech rather than keyboarding to be used as input, will be the managerial or non-typing population. The software will be capable of assisting the processor to distinguish between sound-alike words, such as "their" and "there." The Kurzweil Company, recognized for their development of OCR capability, has developed a prototype of a voice-actuated terminal (VAT).[2] In its early development, the prototype featured a 10,000-word vocabulary and a processing speed of 150 words per minute. Before the machine is used, however, the user must verbalize and record the entire 10,000-word vocabulary so that the machine will recognize the user's voice.

Technology innovators realize that there is, and probably always will be, a large part of the business world that can be

---

[1]Bill Dooley, "Venture a Boost for Videotex," *MIS Week,* 25 April 1984, p. 34.

[2]Bill Dooley, "Typewriter That 'Hears' Lures Wang," *MIS Week,* 3 October, 1984.

classified as "keyboard illiterate"; that is, they do not have touch-typing skills. Some of this is due to the traditional idea that typing is a secretary's work. Though the invasion of the personal computer into the executive's office has done much to alter these attitudes, it is readily accepted that the large volumes of keyboarding will not be an executive's task. While very much in the innovation stages, it is predicted that voice processing will play a major role in the future of office automation.

The first use of voice recognition will most likely occur in the form of voice-actuated commands to a computer, such as commanding the system to PRINT, FILE, RETRIEVE, etc. Such a capability has been marketed by the Votan Company with their VPC 2000 Voice Card. The Voice Card provides complete voice input/output functions for IBM and bus compatible PCs. By incorporating Continuous Speaker-Dependent Recognition (CSDR) capability supplemented with Voice Key Software, users can link sequences of key strokes (up to 30 characters) with previously defined vocabulary. This allows complicated or often used keystrokes to be input by voice commands. In addition to Votan, a number of OA companies are developing voice recognition capability: for example, Digital Equipment Corporation, IBM, Texas Instruments, and Wang.

Another application of voice recognition is through GTE's "Telemessenger" service which was introduced in December of 1984. The service allows a telephone caller to send a voice message in text form. The GTE electronic mail service will enable subscribers to originate text messages and have them delivered in synthetic voice form. The company has provided voice-to-text messages to be delivered via telemail, telex, or other electronic mail services such as MCI Mail or Easylink.

CONTINUING EDUCATION

The importance of staying abreast of technology advances in the information processing field has been mentioned many times throughout this text. The following are suggestions to assist the professional in the continuing education challenge.

Professional Organizations

Join a national professional organization that employs a full-time research staff. In addition to the opportunity to meet other professionals in your field, this type of membership will bring quantities of current technical information to your attention. The membership fee of such organizations is often funded by employers. Of particular importance to the word/information processing industry is the Association of Information Systems Professionals and the Administrative Management Society. Both organizations have national headquarters in Willow Grove, Pennsylvania.

Some of the long established Data Processing organizations, such as Data Processing Management Association and Association for Systems Management, are giving increased attention to word processing topics. The umbrella organization for information processing, the American Federation of Information Processing Society, sponsors the annual National Computer Conference (NCC).

Seminars and Trade Shows

Attend professional seminars and accompanying trade shows. Hundreds of application and industry oriented sessions are held across the United States each year. The National Computer Conference is the largest such trade show, and its seminars are recognized as among the most professional.

Periodicals

Subscribe to appropriate industry magazines and periodicals (see the suggested reading list at the end of this chapter). This affords the best opportunity to keep up to date. The weekly publications offer news of current vendor announcements and technology breakthroughs.

User Groups

Joining "User Groups" can provide the opportunity to share industry knowledge with others in the office automation field.

According to one user group in California, the experience allows for an "informal exchange of ideas and opinions about actual events occurring in companies."[3] Two kinds of user groups are available; user groups for a specific kind of equipment, and general groups that discuss information processing solutions.

TRENDS IN IMPROVING COMPUTER LITERACY

Corporations have become aware of the importance of keeping their employees updated in the information processing disciplines. The Firestone Tire and Rubber Company has established their own internal microcomputer store concept where employees are given technical assistance with "configuration planning (both hardware and software), applications development support, and feasibility studies . . . for microcomputers."[4] In yet another new trend, Boeing Computer Services of Vienna, Virginia offers on-site computer training at the customer's location.[5] This innovative movement to provide information services outside traditional data processing centers, and the efforts of manufacturers to support computer literacy through traditional education channels is examined here.

Information Centers

In the early 1980s, due to the overwhelming acceptance of the PC to suppy processing power to the desktop, MIS managers began to lose some of their control over data processing applications. But more important was the proliferation of multi-vendor PCs purchased by individuals, and their subsequent requests for training, applications assistance and communications to the mainframe computers of their organization.

In answer to these requests, the concept of "Information

---

[3]Rick Minicucci, "West Coast Group Brings OA Down to Earth," *Today's Office*, June 1982, p. 29.

[4]Mike Egan, "Firestone: Implementing a Micro Strategy," *Micro Manager*, Supplement to MIS Week, April 1984, p. 11.

[5]"Boeing Offers CPU Training," *MIS Week*, 9 May, 1984.

Centers" or "I Centers" was created to provide the latest computer hardware and software tools, along with guidance and training for company personnel.[6] Normally staffed with thoroughly trained technical personnel, the I Center provides a resource for employees to perform their own DP or WP tasks, as well as a solution resource and problem solving center. A typical center would be equipped with graphics, spreadsheet, data bases, PCs, microfilm readers, communications and sophisticated printers.

Classroom Training

The importance of computer literacy is exhibited by an announcement of the Digital Equipment Corporation (DEC), providing a cooperative program with the University of Houston to establish "the largest and most advanced computer-intensive education environment in the nation."[7] Grants of up to $35 million will be provided to the University of Houston to establish an Ethernet local area network for some 4,500 personal computers.

Business and industry are not the only social entities embarking in new directions to increase computer literacy. Students in District 50 of Adams County, Colorado are now required to take a course in computer science before they can graduate from high school.[8] In similar action, the public school system in Lowell, Massachusetts has embarked on a computer literacy program that will affect some 6,500 students beginning at the kindergarten years through high school.[9]

Industry Publications

The following list is a sample of the many worthwhile business publications available. Some of the publications are sent free to

---

[6]William M. Cowan, "The 'I Center'—An Office Resource Comes of Age," *Office Administration and Automation*, February 1984, p. 30.

[7]"Houston U, DEC Join In Project," *MIS Week*, 13 June, 1984, p. 6.

[8]"Video terminal awareness: Westminister students like required computer course," *The Daily Sentinel*, Grand Junction, CO, 2 November, 1983, p. 5.

[9]Bill Dooley, "Lowell's Tots Getting CPUs," *MIS Week*, 4 April, 1984, p. 32.

individuals who are actively involved in office automation disciplines.

Computer Systems News. Published weekly by CMP Publications, 111 East Shore Road, Manhasset, NY 11030.

Data Management: The Magazine for the Information Management Executive. Published monthly by the Data Processing Management Association, 505 Busse Highway, Park Ridge, IL 60068–3188.

Datamation. Published monthly by Technical Publishing, a company of The Dun and Bradstreet Corp., 875 Third Avenue, New York, NY 10022.

Datapro Reports and Books. Published by Datapro Research Corporation, 1805 Underwood Boulevard, Delran, NY 08075.

Journal of Data Education. Dr. E. Dana Givson, Executive Director, San Diego State College, San Diego, CA 92115.

Management Information Systems Week (MIS). Published weekly by Fairchild Publications. Available through Circulation Department, MIS Week, P.O. Box 1003, Manasquan, NJ 08736.

Management World: Magazine of the Administrative Management Society. Published monthly by the society, 2360 Maryland Road, Willow Grove, PA 19090.

Modern Office Procedures. Published monthly, P.O. Box 95759, Cleveland, OH 44104.

Office Administration and Automation: The Operations Magazine for Administrative and Systems Executives. Published monthly by Geyer-McAllister Publications, Inc., 51 Madison Avenue, New York, NY 10010.

The Secretary. National Secretaries Ass'n. 2440 Pershing Road, Kansas City, MO 64108.

The Seybold Report on Office Systems. Published monthly by Seybold Publications, Inc., Box 644, Media, PA 19063.

The Seybold Report on Professional Computing. Published monthly by Seybold Publications, Inc., Box 644, Media, PA 19063.

Today's Office: For the Business Operations Manager. Published monthly by Hearst Business Communications, Inc./UPT Division, 645 Stewart Avenue, Garden City, NY 11530.

Words: The Journal of the Association of Information Systems Professionals. Published bimonthly by the Association, 1015 North York Road, Willow Grove, PA 19090.

AISP also publishes a wide variety of technical and industry related materials which are available through special membership rates or for non-members. A complete list of these publications can be ordered by contacting the association at the above address.

DISCUSSION QUESTIONS

1. What type of OA career steps are available to employees of your college or university?

2. Using a copy of the local yellow pages, research the OA support companies listed in your college area.

3. Research one of the industry publications in your college library and make a list of the trade shows occurring within the next six months. Write for information from the sponsoring organizations.

4. What types of support services could be used as a basis for starting your own company?

Glossary of Terms

TERM	*DEFINITION*

access hole   The hole below the spindle hole where the write/read head contacts the diskette.

accounts payable   A liability account in the Statement of Condition into which is recorded the ordinary short-term business payables to outside persons or firms.

accounts receivable   An asset account in the Statement of Condition into which is recorded the amounts owing from outside interests, usually from sales or services performed.

acoustic coupler   A computer connected device into which a telephone handset will fit and which gives and receives audible signals for transmission over a standard telephone line.

adjust   *Word Processing:* A manual action taken to fit text into available space or an automatic function of the equipment to arrange text within designated margins. *Accounting:* Generally an alteration entry to a prior journal entry.

AISP   Association for Information Systems Professionals, successor to IWP (International Word Processing), and one of the largest membership organizations for word/information professionals.

alphanumeric   Includes any or all word processing characters that are either in the set of numbers 0 through 9 or a letter of the alphabet.

alternate format   The secondary format, when two formats have been established for processing text in a given document, and where either can be selected at a given time.

alternate keyboard   The ability to select more than one keyboard character arrangement.

alternating footers   The placement of footer information such as page, title, or similar information in the lower left corner of one page and lower right on the next, generally on pages that are facing each other.

alternating headers   Placement of titles, chapters, section names, etc. at the upper left on one page and upper right on the next, similar to alternating footers.

analog   One of the two basic types of electronic communication signals, i.e., digital and analog. Analog signals are distinguished by the height and length of waves in a continuous signal.

ANSI   American National Standards Institute, the organization composed of industry representatives which sets all types of standards by voluntary action and publishes them for use by anyone wishing to follow them.

application   A single computer task, such as invoicing, or financial analysis, which may consist of one program or a family of programs. It is usually documented as one unit.

archive   In use as either a noun, verb, or adjective in references to the retention of information in any medium separate from, and usually in a more secure location than, data readily available in a processing environment.

arithmetic/logic unit   That part of the processor containing the circuits that perform arithmetic and logic.

ASCII

American Standard Code for Information Interchange. Set by ANSI, it is the standardized recording of 128 alphanumeric and other characters, as punched holes or digital representatives in data processing media.

asynchronous communication

One of the two methods of moving data in telecommunications; each character is identified at its beginning and end as it enters and leaves the communication line. (See Binary Synchronous Communication)

automation

The process or establishment of functions carried out without human involvement. Automation can be expressed as percentages, as in 50% automated.

background printing

A processor capability whereby printing of one or several documents can be taking place while other, completely separate tasks can be done at the keyboard (in the foreground).

background processing

Similar to background printing except that processing such as sorting or communication is carried out while the keyboard is being used in the foreground.

backup diskette

A duplicate diskette of valuable information to be used should the original diskette become unusable for any reason.

bandwidth

A designation of the quality of transmission facilities without distortion. A voice band communication system or line will accommodate a wider range of frequencies than will a narrow band line.

BASIC

A computer programming source language developed at Dartmouth College in 1963 by Professors Kemeny & Kurtz, which has become widely used in all sizes of computers.

batch processing

The processing of all of an activity at one time, such as the once-a-month processing of invoices, as contrasted with processing each transaction, such as a sale, as it occurs.

baud	A measure of communication speed on a per second basis, such as the individual binary portions of a character (bit) per second; e.g., 200 baud would mean 200 such portions per second.
benchmark	The accomplishment of specifically identified hardware or software which is used as a basis for comparison to other similar facilities.
bidirectional printing	Printing that minimizes carrier return time by merely line feeding at either end of a printed line and printing the succeeding line in the reverse direction. Each line is pre-assembled in the processor so that it spaces correctly whether printed right to left or left to right.
binary code	The use of a series of electric pulses, punched holes, magnetized positions or any other recording where a condition can be only one of two possibilities, for identifying characters of information.
binary synchronous communication	Also called bisynch or merely synchronous, in contrast to *asynchronous*, this type of communication is higher speed in that synchronization occurs each second as data is transmitted.
black box	Though used occasionally in reference to a computer, it most often refers to an in-line device within a communication link which alters data signals in such a way that the sending and receiving stations are compatible.
block move	The movement of information in a block or grouping, other than a word, a sentence, a paragraph, etc., and in which the operator or the system arbitrarily designates the length of the block and the location to which it is moved.
boilerplate	Standard or repetitive information for a contract or other document which is stored in a word processing system for insertion at a later time, relieving the task of re-keyboarding.

boldface   A printing function in which each character prints twice, the second impression sometimes slightly to one side of the original strike, causing a bolder appearance.

broadband   One of the three classes of transmission lines. The classifications range from narrow band with the narrowest range, to voice band with the middle speed ranges, and broadband which can handle the ranges of the other two and higher.

bubble memory   A type of crystal memory which can process at very high speeds but generally with less flexibility than the silicon chip.

buffer   A limited sized, special purpose memory unit within a computer system, whose purpose is to substantially speed processing. It is generally used in conjunction with data input and output.

burst speed   Term sometimes used to describe typing as fast as possible without concern for errors, coding, or carriage returns. Also refers to the top speed of certain recording devices which operate intermittently.

captured keystrokes   Sometimes called stored keystrokes, it is a capability for setting aside phrases, formulas, paragraphs, or any key combination for keyboarding, playout, and printing on an as-requested basis.

cartridge   A container of either a reel of tape or one or more disks, which can be removed from the processing system.

cassette   A small plastic unit of narrow magnetic tape used in recording either sound or data for later playback or retrieval.

cathode ray tube   (CRT) The television-type screen with either single or multi-color display used in conjunction with keyboard operations.

central processing unit Used in two references, it can either be the internal component of a computer through which data and program instructions flow, or the entire central fixture with attached keyboard and printer.

centralized dictation A recording system on a telephone dial-up connection within an organization for use in dictating material to be typed.

character per second (CPS) A measure used to express the printing speed of a character printer.

circuit board A flat surface object with permanently printed or molded electrical circuits and fixtures, which can be either added to or replaced within a computer.

coded function The functions within word or data processing that are activated by pressing two or more keys in combination. When multiple keys are used, one is generally either a CODE key or CONTROL key.

column layout A function or coded function which automatically establishes column spacing for text or numerical applications.

combined program disk The placement of multiple programs or applications onto one disk to minimize diskette handling while processing. This is particularly practiced where the system diskette unit is of multiple density.

communications The clear transfer and receipt of data and their meanings from one person, group, place or facility to another, either by voice or via electronic medium.

compatibility Refers, in information processing, to the similarity of code makeup, media size, program language, ratio of speed, parameters, or any other factors allowing or restricting joint functioning of equipment.

computer program
An array or sequence of instructions which cause a computer to accomplish a task. A program is originated in source language understandable to the programmer and then converted (compiled) into a language (object) understandable by the particular computer.

concept
The approach taken to achieve a particular function or feature.

continuous form
Single or layered paper in a continuous roll with perforations for separating the paper into individual pages at intervals. The paper can be blank, lined, or imprinted with a format. Small holes in the right and left edges accommodate sprocket pins of the printer for accurate paper feeding.

control program for microcomputers
Commonly called CP/M, this software, created and copyrighted by Digital Research, Inc., was one of the earliest and is among the most widely used small computer operating systems.

conversational mode
A form of software operation in which there is a continuing interchange between the computer and operator, with the computer responses occurring almost immediately. Also used to describe a direct "on-line" message interchange between computer operators.

copy
1) A duplicate of all or part of the contents of another similar or different medium; 2) A process of producing a duplicate; 3) Second and succeeding pages in a multi-part form.

CPU
See Central Processing Unit.

CRT
See Cathode Ray Tube.

cursor
On a CRT display, a lighted indicator of the current location of interest to the operator, either as a result of the operator's actions or as program prompting.

daisy wheel A type of printer element, so named because it resembles a daisy. A print character is located at the end of each extension from the center. It is easily exchanged on the printer for another daisy wheel with a different type style or font.

data The information, regardless of whether alphabetic or numeric and whether text or other information, for which programs are designed to accept, manipulate and otherwise read, write, store, and process.

data base In its narrowest context, it is a single file of information of a particular type, such as employee data; in the broadest context all of the data of all files in an organization. Sophisticated programming is often used in the arrangement and handling of data bases.

data entry The introduction of data into a processor by any of several methods, by far the more common being by keyboard. The term is also used to describe the preparation of a source document for later keying.

data processing Includes all functioning of a computer or information processor, although sometimes not intended to include text processing. See Word Processing.

decimal tab One of the types of tabulating functions in word processing providing the automatic alignment of numbers around a decimal point.

dedicated line 1) An A/C power line from a building's power panel serving only one outlet point; 2) A telephone line within an organization, free of all switching and serving only one connecting point.

dedicated printer One not available for use by more than one processor or terminal.

dedicated processor A processor which is permanently equipped basically to perform word processing only.

de facto standard   A facility, method, or measurement which has evolved as the standard through wide usage and natural preference.

default   Decisions designed into software; these frequently reflect standards of an industry involved in the software.

default format   Standards for the printed page such as line length, page length, characters per inch, etc.

delete   To remove characters, lines, records, or other such groupings from further program accessibility. Deletions often do not result in actual physical removal from a disk or diskette other than from the directory.

demodulation   Conversion of analog to digital signals. See Modem.

density   The number of bits per inch of track on which information can be placed on a tape or disk medium. Density is expressed as single, dual, or quad.

disc   Also *disk*. Used as a reference for any type of flat, round, rotating medium with concentric recording tracks on one or both surfaces. Data is placed upon and read with a read/write head for each recording surface.

disk drive   Equipment which holds and revolves disks and which contains the read/write heads for placing and accessing data.

diskette   A type of flexible disk which is permanently encased in a protective envelope or covering and revolves within its covering when in use. Provides for the external storage of information. It is generally easily removable from its disk drive.

diskette drive   A disk drive for diskettes.

diskette slot   The opening in the outer covering of a diskette drive through which a diskette is inserted into the drive.

distributed logic   See *distributed processing.*

distributed processing   Refers to a combination of computer systems in which there is a central primary system connected to a network of secondary computers, each with independent processing capability and with independent data storage. Master data, processed data and program logic are interchanged.

distributed system   See *distributed processing.*

document   As either a noun or verb, makes reference to the existence or placement of information in a manner which can be held, read by people, and filed; usually involves a paper product.

document assembly   The internal gathering of previously produced or previously keyboarded portions of a document into a finished document for printing or storing.

document format   The stored decisions that reflect the operator's decisions for all physical characteristics of a document, such as page length, line length, spacing, etc.

documentation   Descriptive information and user instructions concerning computer software or processing applications.

dot matrix   A method of printing and of CRT display in which characters are formed in a manner similar to the rectangles of lights on a sporting event scoreboard. The rectangle of data nearly always contains more lines of dots from top to bottom than from side to side.

dual column   More than one column of text on a page, each with a uniform left margin. Some printing equipment prints all columns at a time as each line is printed. Others print a full column and return the paper to the top for printing of the next column.

duplicate

See *copy.*

EDP

Electronic data processing. See *data processing.*

electronic communication

See *communications.*

electronic mail

The deployment of terminals and the arrangement of software in an organization in such a way that correspondence is communicated, stored, and retrieved electronically, with only a minimum of actual paper movement.

electronic wastebasket

Term applied to a section on a disk designed by software to store deleted material.

emulation

Through software, a processing system takes on all of the characteristics of processing by a different system. Often an older, formerly owned system is emulated so that prior programs do not need to be replaced.

ergonomics

Design factors for enhancement of human usage.

external storage

A medium of information storage which can be physically removed from an information processor and separately handled, shipped, or safeguarded.

facsimile

Communication of an exact photo or image of a document, the duplicate at the receiving end being termed the facsimile.

facsimile transmission

The process of communicating a facsimile.

feasibility study   A study or examination made preliminary to any other work on a project to determine costs, time and people involvement, benefits, and targets, to ascertain whether there is agreement to proceed with the actual project.

field   A single unit of information within a data record; such as birthdate within an employee record.

field engineers   Computer maintenance personnel.

file   *Data and Record Processing:* The total collection of a particular type of record. For example, the collection of all employee records would constitute an employee file. *Word Processing:* Retained text in word processing is generally referred to as a document rather than a file.

find   Sometimes used as the search function, and generally used as the result of either the find or search functions when an exact match is obtained.

fixed disk   A disk that cannot be physically removed from a system. The capacity and revolving speed are generally greater than in removable disks. See *disc.*

floppy disk   See *diskette.*

format display   An option on some word processors providing the display of coding on the CRT representing format settings, such as margins, tabs, carrier returns, etc.

function   Widely used in EDP, mathematics, business, and other fields to represent a single process, a grouping or a totality of related steps. An umbrella term in WP incorporating all automatic capabilities of the equipment.

function keys   Keys designated to perform a single process or function, such as a *delete* key.

global search   A search from the point of the cursor location for a specified group of characters. In some systems, the search ends at the first encounter, and in others all occurrences of the characters are searched.

global search and replace   Similar to *global search* except that a replacement set of characters is given to put in place of the search characters found.

glossary   Reference used in some word processing systems for captured keystrokes. See *captured keystrokes.*

go to   A function of rapidly moving the cursor to a specific location and the display of requested point of reference material on the CRT.

graphics   Computerized production either on the CRT or on hard copy of pictures, graphs, or charts.

hard carriage return   Code result of the operator pressing the carriage return key.

hard copy   A printout on paper of the contents of a computer medium.

hard disk   See *fixed disk.*

hard sector   A diskette which has more than one index hole. The diskette is written on by means of sensing and timing when writing, and also when reading.

hardware   Tangible processing equipment, as contrasted with software, which is the programming that is used to direct the equipment process.

hardwired system   An internal program which is permanent and integral to the system.

hyphenation

Also termed *hyphenation pass,* it is the process of dividing words into two parts by accepted rules where the word is at the end of a line and extends beyond the established right margin.

impact printer

A printer that makes its imprints by striking a character against the paper or ribbon, as contrasted with a photograph, heat, or spray process.

index hole

The small 1/10-inch hole (or holes) which allows the diskette drive to determine the starting point to sector the disk when writing or reading.

index tract

Tract 00 (last outside track of a diskette) is called the index track, and is reserved for information which describes the contents of the disk.

information processing

The inclusive realm of computerized data processing and word processing; can be interpreted to include all office automation devices that process information.

initialize

1) Startup process such as turning on equipment, setting registers to start points, or loading a control program. 2) Preparation process such as erasing the contents and setting the format of a diskette.

ink-jet printer

A printer which produces character images on paper by spraying ink through very small apertures at the paper. Speed attained is in the high range of letter quality printers.

insert mode

A function to place additional characters between existing ones required on some processors.

intelligent terminal

A terminal connected by some type of communication line to a primary computer, where the secondary computer is capable of functioning either independently or in conjunction with the primary computer. A terminal which can only work with the primary computer's programs is frequently referred to as a *dumb terminal.*

interactive video   Software, used frequently in training, in which an operator's responses are required during its functioning. The interaction is considered conversational in nature.

internal memory   See *memory*.

IWP   The predecessor to AISP.

job   A total task of related steps, such as the running of one program or the running of combined programs and utility steps as one controlled flow of work.

justification   Text printing which has a straight even margin on both right and left sides. The equal length of all lines is attained by the alteration of spacing within each line.

key-to-print   A word processing procedure where printing occurs immediately as each key is depressed. Neither editing nor retention occur.

keyboard   The computer input facility containing all character keys as well as the associated function keys.

keyboarding   The process of inputting from a keyboard. Also called key entering.

keystrokes   WP terminology for the typing of characters.

LAN   Local Area Network. The direct interconnection of computerized equipment by cables or wires for interchange of processing throughout the network.

laser   An incorporation of laser technology into a computerized process; e.g., a laser printer. Laser technology involves light generation using certain mineral crystals.

library   1) A named area on disk that can contain programs, constants, text statements, or procedures which are incorporated into processing on an as needed basis. 2) Users create their own library of stored documents, usually through a combination of their ID and password.

licensed programs   Progams which are provided at a cost to the user under copyright protection to the manufacturer.

linking   A method of combining documents during printing.

list processing   A limited type of records processing in which a stored list of names or names and addresses or descriptions are processed by themselves or in combination with text.

local area network   See LAN.

machine language   A computer program in a language understood by a specific machine. Machine language programs are generally produced by the computer from the programmer's source language program, being processed through a special program called a compiler.

mag card   A card storage medium in the shape of a standard punched card, made of durable plastic, and coated with magnetic material. It is used in word processing equipment designed for processing that medium of storage.

magnetic disk, diskette   See *diskette, disc.*

magnetic media   Any of the various forms of materials such as cards, disks, tapes, or inks with recording surfaces or integral properties which can be magnetized selectively and retain the magnetization for equipment sensing.

magnetic tape   A plastic, flexible tape produced in widths from 1/8-inch to over an inch, and lengths up to many hundreds of feet, or in some cases continuous, with a magnetic coating on one surface for storing audio, video, or data recordings.

main menu   In a computerized system involving menu control, it is the starting menu, the menu to which control is returned following completion of an optional application.

mainframe   Any of the class of large computers which are generally capable of extensive communication and networking, multi-programming and large media and storage handling.

matrix   A two-dimensional array of points used in printed and CRT character representations and in certain mathematical and scientific applications.

media converter   Equipment designed to read information from one type of media and reproduce the information onto another medium; e.g., conversion of punch cards to diskettes.

memory   An internal equipment capability for receiving information, retaining it, and giving access to it. RAM (Random Access Memory) can be erased and overwritten with new information, which it then stores for access. ROM (Read Only Memory) cannot be erased or overwritten in normal processing.

menu   A software-produced listing on the CRT from which alternatives of processing can be selected.

menu-driven software   Program systems which have alternatives of processing and which incorporate menu selection as the basis for choosing the alternatives by the operator.

merge Combining of files into one under specified condition. Usually the files being merged are sequenced in a given manner. Merge is used extensively in computer sorting operations.

microcassette A very small cassette, generally considered the smallest in data recording use.

microcomputer The hierarchy of computer size classifications is Personal Computer; Microcomputer; Minicomputer; and Mainframe, from smallest to largest, respectively. There is overlapping of characteristics from one to another.

microprocessor The internal central component of a small computer through which and by which all processing takes place. Usually a silicon chip.

minicomputer See *microcomputer.*

mnemonic A coding scheme designed with association characteristics for easy memory of the code's function or meaning. Codes of 1 and 2 for Add and Subtract would not be mnemonic, whereas A and S would be.

modem A device for converting voice type signals used in telecommunications to digital signals used in most computers and vice versa. Combination of *MO*dulator/*DEM*odulator.

modulation Conversion of digital to analog signals. See *modem.*

move A function of deleting specified information from its present position and relocating it to a new location. Different from COPY, where deleting does not take place.

OCR Optical character recognition. The reading (scanning) of alphabetic, numeric, and certain other characters by machine, and placing the characters on a different medium. A special standard set of printed characters has been developed for OCR.

office automation Machines accomplishing clerical and administrative tasks formerly accomplished by people.

operating system A special type of software which must be in a computer for it to operate and which controls all of the hardware functions.

operator 1) A person using equipment. 2) A portion of an instruction in machine language programs.

outline function Automated spacing and indenting in an outline format available in some word processing systems.

overstrike A function in some word processing systems providing for a second different character to be placed over those already there for reference during editing.

pagination Automatic delineation of page endings in keyboarded text. Special rules for first and last paragraph lines are applied in some word processing systems.

paper tape A medium in which data is recorded by punched holes in paper tape of 3/4-inch width.

password A string of characters that, when entered with a user identification, allows an operator to sign on to the system.

peripherals Excluding the keyboard, peripherals include any equipment attached to a central processor, such as a printer.

**personal
computer**

See *microcomputer.*

photocomposition   Used in the printing industry, a primary step in converting source-typed text into typeset masters from which print plates are made for presses.

pitch   Type spacing per inch horizontally on a typed line. For example, 12 pitch indicates 12 characters, or spaces, per inch.

playback   With application primarily to the earliest word processing equipment, it is the printing of a proof copy from a recorded memory such as a mag card.

portability   The capability of using, on one equipment facility, the data or programs created, used, or written on another.

prerecorded   Text that has been previously keyboarded and saved on a medium for later use.

print   The process of placing characters on a surface which will allow them to be read by humans.

productivity   The ratio or relationship of the quantity of produced goods or services to the amount of labor time expended in its production.

program   Instructions to be used by a computer for carrying out a specific task. There are essentially two forms of programs. A program is first developed in a programming language (source) and then converted to a machine language (object). Many different object programs (for different machines) can be produced from one source program.

**programming
language**

A vocabulary of acceptable terms and a specified format (together called *syntax*), for writing instructions to be carried out by a computer.

proportional spacing A type of printing in which the printer is capable of very small spacing increments and in which the amount of printing space provided for each character is in relation to the size of the character. For example, *M* is given much more space for printing than *i*.

punched card A medium for recording information in which small rectangular holes are punched in rows and columns in a standardized piece of thin cardboard.

RAM See *memory*.

random access Any medium or memory in which any location can be accessed, or gone to, directly, as contrasted with tape or most card memory in which the reading must proceed from the beginning.

read-only See *memory*.

records processing In word processing, the processing of information in a file type of structure either by itself or in conjunction with text.

records search The accessing of selected records in a file on the basis of qualifying criteria.

remote terminal A terminal facility that is connected to the primary computer through some type of communication other than a direct cable.

revision The process of altering previously keyboarded information by deleting, relocating, adding, or combinations of the three.

right justify See *justification*.

ROM See *memory*.

scan Any of various processes of looking at or listening to previously recorded information. Also see OCR.

search capability A machine capability for scanning the contents of stored records and comparing them to given characters to find desired records.

setup A common term in word processing to describe the format and characteristics of a document.

shared logic system Local or remote terminals in a communication arrangement with a primary computer in which only the primary computer has the capability of processing programs and the other terminals can receive the results of that processing.

shared printer A printer which provides the printing function for more than one processor. Generally one processor acts as the control unit and queuing base.

shared resource system A system in which certain or all resources such as disk storage or printers are accessed by all of the computers in a communication hook-up.

shell document A document format prepared for merging and printing text or file information previously recorded.

soft carriage return Code definition for carriage return resulting from the automatic carriage return function.

soft sector A diskette which has only one index hole. The disk needs to be electronically formatted before use.

software Programming or programs of all kinds.

software house   A business which deals in programs, either as author, vendor, consultant, or services.

spelling check   A computerized verification of the spelling accuracy of a keyboarded document, either as keyboarded or at the completion of the document or individual pages.

spindle hole   The hole in the center of the disk.

stand-alone system   A computerized system that includes the total information processing and printing capability, sharing neither the logic nor the resources of another system.

switch code   *Word Processing:* A code inserted in text which directs the processor to access an alternate source or go back to the original. *Data Processing:* Data codes that can be set into memory by the operator or a program to give processing direction through subsequent accessing.

system analysis   A general term of human activity which encompasses a review of present computerized and manual methods and procedures, changes desired or needed, programming requirements, cost analysis, and testing and implementing. The actual programming activity may or may not be included.

task analysis   A process to determine the most productive method(s) to produce a document or project.

telecommunications   Distribution of information via telephone lines, telegraph, radio or other electro-magnetic means. Also see *communications.*

teleconferencing   Telephone conversation involving more than two telephone stations; generally implies relatively long physical distances between the parties.

teletypewriter The use of equipment of Teletype Corporation for the communication of text or various types of messages, usually through the communication facilities of Western Union corporation.

telex A message sent on a Teletype machine.

text In the general area of information processing, text involves words, messages, sentences, and related documents, whereas data incorporates numerics, accounting, statistics, and the like.

text editing The review and alteration or revision of text.

track A circular recording path on the diskette surface.

underscore Also called *underline,* it is the placement of a horizontal line under words, a function provided or automated by most word processing software, but in many different ways.

user The person operating a processing facility or the person or group receiving the benefits or services of the processing performed.

user group An organization or society of persons or companies whose common bond is their ownership or other possession of a particular type or brand of processing equipment. Some such organizations are nationwide in membership.

user-friendly system Generally applies to either hardware or software which is not confusing, overly complicated, nor unreasonably technical for the user or operator to realize desired results.

VDT Video display terminals; see *cathode ray tube* (CRT).

vendor

A marketer of products. In information processing it is commonly used in reference to brand or manufacturer.

virtual memory

A type of processing control, particularly in mini or larger computers, whereby portions or entire programs are moved between internal and external memory during processing, thus providing capacity for more programs to be processed at one time.

voice recognition

Direct recognition of human voice statements by a computer sufficient for processing, thus eliminating any type of keyboarding as the input method.

windowing

The placement of more than one screen image on a CRT at one time, either by the images sharing the screen or with one or more images overlaying the others.

winchester disk drive

Early models of the internal hard disk storage units contained two disk drives, each having the capacity of 30 megabytes. The name "Winchester," referring to the old "30–30 rifle," was a natural consequence. Also, see *fixed disk.*

word processing

Text processing, as generally contrasted with data processing.

words per minutes (WPM)

A measure used in defining the keyboarding speed of an operator.

work diskette

Diskettes are often used either as Program Diskettes into which software has been recorded, or Work Diskettes which are used to record data or documents. Work Diskettes are generally designated or classified by purpose or user and secured in keeping with the importance or sensitivity of the contents.

write/read (or Parity)

The process of recording. The information is written and then read back to be sure that information is not written on a bad spot.

Appendix

DP AND WP: THE BEST LAID PLANS*

By Joyce Fassl

Millions of office workers learn how to operate new data processing and word processing systems every day. But, despite corporate planning and good intentions to streamline office work, man and machine often mix like water and oil.

One large Canadian company, Petro-Canada, did all its homework, but still came up short in one of its office automation systems conversions.

The large government-owned research and refining company began a company-wide office automation plan. A progressive vice president at Petro-Canada believed that effective office automation systems must integrate word processing, data processing and communications.

But before an office automation plan could be put into action, the company had to look inside itself and answer some key questions. Is the present wp system really being used properly? Is training adequate? How well are data processing and word processing integrated?

How do people adapt to a new system after working on the same one for several years? What can managers and supervisors do to ease the conversion pain?

After careful consideration an overall plan was developed to integrate office automation throughout the company. Management put an emphasis on user training and hired professional trainers who conducted systems refresher courscs.

The conversion team developed a company newsletter featuring articles on office automation, word processing, a "Did You Know" column, and an "Ask Wordy" column.

---

*Reprinted with permission from *Words* Magazine: *The Journal of the Association of Information Systems Professionals* (June–July, 1984).

Four departments were chosen to participate in pilots. The pilots were proceeding as planned, except for one department.

All But One

This department was one area where wp and dp systems needed to be integrated. Operators there key in rather technical documents such as statistical reports and spread sheets. With the previous system, the operators used two different terminals—one for word processing and one for data processing. The conversion consisted of going from the standalone system with different terminals to a shared logic system. The new system would let the operators key in word and data processing on the same terminal.

The department went from an easy-to-learn-and-use system to a more complex system. It was mostly for data processing, but had wp capabilities. This dp bias made it more difficult because most of the users were used to a system that favored word processing.

Although the new system was powerful, the employees found it very difficult to use. The new system required the operators to learn a series of codes for word processing, the basic need of the department. Although the operators had to key complicated codes in the previous system, the new codes seemed even more complicated. There was a lot of pressure to learn the new codes, thus adding to the difficulty of the entire process.

"The new system turned out to be more like a dp system than a wp system," according to Carol Lukasiewich, Petro-Canada support trainer. She said that the previous system seemed easier to the operators because of the difficult codes in the new system.

Elspeth Eldred, Petro-Canada project leader for text management systems, adds "People tend to like the first system they ever worked with. They are constantly comparing their first system experience to the one they have now."

Management Support Lags

Petro-Canada also had to deal with some internal conflicts during this conversion. Management interest and support in this particular installation was lacking. Operators within the department had no sense of team spirit and seemed to work very independently. The employees' reaction to training sessions was negative because of attitude problems and the difficulty of learning the complicated codes. Also, none of the users were asked for their opinions prior to the conversion.

Another problem Petro-Canada faced was with the vendor. The vendor itself was unfamiliar with the system and had to refer to other branch offices for answers to Petro-Canada's questions. "At one point during the pilot, the system was down for an entire day," Eldred said. And in the company's eyes this was disastrous.

Later, a complete company reorganization and relocation plan was put into action. A system successfully used in another pilot within the company was introduced in the department. This, coupled with the move to the new Petro-Canada headquarters, proved to be the antidote the department needed.

What's a Company to Do?

The best way to conduct an office automation systems conversion is planning, according to Eldred. She also stated that it is important to sell the managers and supervisors involved on the qualities of the new system. Another overlooked key part of planning is the involvement of the operators.

"Make sure people know all about the conversion—including the advantages of the new system, what they need to learn to operate the new equipment, the conversion time frames, and who and where they can get the answers they need," Eldred says.

Eldred stresses the importance of a conversion plan. A typical plan in use at Petro-Canada runs for three months. The plan includes vendor selection, laying the wire, the actual installation, and training. She also stresses the importance of having an expert on the premises during the entire conversion process to answer all questions from the operators.

Petro-Canada's training course consists of vendor material tailored to a particular department's needs.

To get the operators involved in the conversion, Eldred suggests forming a team that includes users, a management representative and a systems expert (Petro-Canada uses an in-house trainer) and keeping everyone informed of all aspects.

"The amount of education given to the principal is tremendously important," states Eldred. She also states the amount of education time given to the users will also make them feel very confident with the system.

Humans vs. Machines

Although Eldred thinks that much of the problem in this conversion resulted from human rather than machine problems, she admits that there were systems problems. But she said that with the correct planning and training, many of the problems "probably could have been overcome."

Lukasiewich's advice for office automation systems conversion is to keep everyone informed.

"As soon as you know you are getting a new system, let the operators know." Also, she suggests letting them know the conversion schedule and making as many presentations and demonstrations as possible.

She believes in letting the operators be involved directly with the conversion if possible. Ask for their ideas. The more involved they are, the better they will feel about learning the new equipment, she feels.

Another way Petro-Canada combats office automation problems is with a wp strategy used to develop lists of potential vendors. Through this strategy they identified two vendors who meet the needs of the entire company. Petro-Canada can call on either of these two vendors, who are familiar with the needs of the company, without going through a series of vendor selections.

Despite the problems Petro-Canada faced in this particular conversion, things are now going well with the new system in place. To address future office automation needs, Petro-Canada has developed an ongoing office automation plan. Based on lessons learned in past pilots, they are striving to make man and machine work effectively and efficiently.

Office automation system conversions are rarely simple. Frequently, it is difficult to gain cooperation from all the people involved. But if a company can achieve the right balance of planning, organizing and training, an office automation conversion need not be so painful.

Comments of article's author follow:

Rx for Conversion Cure

- Draw up a plan and follow it.
- Form a team that includes users, manager and trainer.
- Ask for user suggestions.
- Organize documents and label diskettes.
- Conduct presentations and demonstrations.
- Provide training and continued education.

Petro-Canada, owned by the Canadian government, is an energy industry leader in research, drilling, production, refining, and distribution. In April of 1981, the information systems and services department joined with the administrative services department to develop an office automation system strategy for the entire corporation.

One of Petro-Canada's departments, with a staff of 50, needed a system with both wp and dp capabilities. The wp system successfully used in the company's legal department is now installed in this and other departments with equal success.

The original office automation project team was reorganized into the text management systems department headed by Elspeth Eldred. The department develops training seminars and plans new installations. Eldred's group works to avoid the types of problems the company experienced in past installations.

By establishing the text management systems department to oversee office automation pilots and conversions, Petro-Canada is producing an efficient and effective workplace.

HOW LAW FIRM UPGRADED WP OPERATIONS*

By Toni S. Larocque

About two years ago, a growing work load prompted our law firm to take a close look at our word processing operations. At that time, one wp center served the firm's 150 attorneys. The center consisted of an IBM System 6 with three terminals and a laser printer. In addition, 25 of the 90 secretaries had mag card machines.

Requirements

It was obvious that the mag card machines were outdated and unable to handle sophisticated applications, and that the wp center was unable to handle increasingly heavy work loads.

To lay the ground work for our study, the support manager talked with all attorneys and secretaries, explained the value of their input, and stressed that their honest feedback was critical in the development of an accurate picture of the law firm's type and volume of work.

The law firm then contacted a consultant to interview the secretaries and study their work habits. The systems support manager worked closely with the consultant and was able to zero in on some key applications that each secretary would perform.

At this stage, we established the criteria a secretary must meet in order to be allocated a terminal. Once these criteria were approved by the firm's executive committee, we sent a questionnaire to secretaries to measure two variables. First, it singled out those secretaries whose typing load was 25 hours

---

*Reprinted with permission from *Format: The Word Processing Newsletter of AISP*, the Association of Information Systems Professionals, Willow Grove, PA (October, 1984).

per week or more. Second, it asked how many documents required retyping to accommodate attorneys' revisions.

System Configuration

We used this data to evauate the options in systems configuration and to allocate systems resources.

Centralization, favored by some, would have configured all word processing equipment in the word processing center. Each of nine departments would have had its own wp specialist in the center dedicated to that department's work.

The analysis led us to choose a distributed word processing configuration over centralization on two points.

First, the cost of hiring the necessary legal wp specialists was less cost effective than the purchase of terminals for 25 secretaries, each of whom would support two to three attorneys. Our analysis took into account decreased typing time, increased productivity, fewer bottlenecks and reduced overtime if each secretary used an advanced wp system.

Secondly, a decentralized approach allows more people to have access to a common data base.

We didn't totally reject the concept of a word processing center, but decided to integrate two approaches in our office automation system—terminals on secretaries' desks and a wp center which would support attorneys whose secretaries did not have terminals.

We searched the market and evaluated several systems based on our established criteria. We selected a shared resource by NBI that could handle many terminals and printers. We also saw the value in using OCR technology.

Pre-Installation Orientation

Before the equipment arrived, we conducted an orientation program for attorneys and secretaries to prep them on terminology, hardware and software. We described the concept of shared resources and familiarized everyone with the manuals that would be used.

We also discussed the prospect of the equipment malfunctioning and stressed back-up and recovery procedures throughout orientation and the training program.

For the secretaries, we stressed similarities between the [IBM] mag cards and the NBI system. For example, the mag card CODE key is equivalent to the ALTSHIFT key on the NBI. You have to depress the CODE key and the WORD UND key to underscore on the mag card, while on the NBI you press ALTSHIFT and UND to underscore.

The System

In three phases we installed two ICUs (Integrated Control Units), the terminals and 14 printers. Each phase occurred at two month intervals to provide a smooth transition.

Our wp center has five terminals, three printers and one OCR scanner. In addition, we have one terminal in the center for training or for solving problems over the phone with secretaries who are using a terminal. This "training" terminal allows one to quickly locate a document while on the phone with a secretary without having to interrupt work in progress on the other terminals in the center.

The center's main responsibility is to serve attorneys whose secretaries do not have a terminal because their typing loads did not warrant one. Initial input is done by the secretaries on their typewriters. Changes are marked in red by the attorney. The document is then submitted to the wp center and scanned by OCR. Since the bulk of the text is recorded on memory via OCR, wp operators only make the revisions noted in red.

Acceptance

In the beginning, some secretaries were intimidated by the new terminals and showed some resistance. Many began to question their skills and felt as if their jobs were on the line. After all, they had been hired as secretaries, not as word processing operators. Although they had experience on the mag card machines, the new system was still something different to them.

But as time went on and training progressed, resistance eroded and the secretaries began to show enthusiasm.

Training

Management made it clear that the secretaries had their full support in wp training and in training for special applications. Attorneys were informed that secretaries would need time to learn how to use the system efficiently. That included time to do the exercises and attend training classes.

The secretaries were encouraged to spend at least two hours per week on the training exercises. The attorney's support was a must, if this were to take place. It is much harder to control the training pace in a distributed environment than in a center where training pressures can be regulated.

Many times a secretary was simply too busy to spend time on exercises and was allowed to work overtime for this purpose. For many, this time worked out even better for training since distractions were eliminated.

It was important to stress to each secretary that she must do the training exercises, but not push herself unnecessarily. Self-pacing was stressed to prevent unhealthy competition among co-workers.

The project manager and assistant developed the in-house training program which consisted of classes two hours per week for six weeks. Each secretary operating a terminal had to attend all classes. There were make-up classes for those who missed a regular class.

Secretaries do not begin the six week course until they have been on the terminal for one week. This way they get the feel of the machine and are able to discuss problems more intelligently in class.

During the first week on a terminal, a secretary is encouraged to do the exercises, record documents originated from the attorneys and experiment with the printer. This helps them become more comfortable with the system and prevents early burn out that can result from too much training too soon.

We also developed a training/operations manual specifically for the law firm. The manual has instructions on formatting a letter, document assembly, printing envelopes, recovery procedures, file management, care and maintenance, etc.

We did allow some secretaries to retain their mag card machines for at least a week while working on their new terminals. If a rush project had to go out in a day, they were not under unusual pressure to learn the new system.

Areas to Watch

We had to consider certain key changes when going to a distributed environment.

Idle terminals. Secretaries have other responsibilities besides keyboarding. The average amount of time they spend on the system each day ranges from three to four and one half hours. Some people feel that if the system is not running all day, that we are not getting our money's worth. But, it is not always feasible to expect maximum utilization of terminals with a distributed system.

Longer learning curves. Since the secretary is not using the system continuously and is not performing as many applications as a wp specialist, the learning curve naturally is longer. In our firm, a wp specialist feels very comfortable with the system by the second or third month. Secretaries often require three to four months.

Equipment handling. Because the law firm is spread throughout four floors, keeping an eye on all the equipment is a large job. (When all equipment is in word processing centers, it is much easier!) Secretaries are asked to turn off peripherals when they leave for lunch or for the day. But, there are always instances when a terminal or printer is left on after hours.

Each ICU, terminal and printer is securely labeled with identification numbers. And to facilitate the movement and placement of peripherals around the building, we label *all* cables. A spec sheet is taped to each of the ICRs for the benefit of the field engineer.

Equipment Security. Our firm's policy states that under no circumstances can a terminal be used by someone who has not been trained on the system. Attorneys and friends of secretaries are sometimes tempted to "play with the new computer."

Service and Maintenance. All service requests must be placed through the systems manager's office. If someone is having trouble with the system, we do our in-house trouble shooting first. Most problems are operator error and not machine error. When a printer is down, secretaries are advised which printer to use.

Platen cleaning is a must. Secretaries are supplied with a bottle of Fedron [Fedron is a trade name of platen cleaner], and are requested to clean platens twice per week. Some need to use it twice per day to solve paper jamming problems.

Document Control and File Management. Management is the key word here. In the training course, wp specialists and secretaries are instructed on file naming, retention and archiving.

Documents are named by file number and date. Each time a secretary begins a job, she must enter the document name and the date in a log kept at the secretary's desk at all times. Temporary personnel will be able to locate jobs quickly when a secretary is absent.

Confidential documents or those over 20 pages are stored on floppy disks, instead of on the system's main memory at the discretion of the secretary. The secretary notifies the wp support center when a job must be archived on the system's memory. [Note: The particular NBI system utilized in this case study allows for internal and external storage of documents; the external storage is accomplished by the system's disk drive onto diskettes.]

Once a week an index of all documents stored on memory is printed and distributed to each secretary, who makes decisions in conjunction with the attorney on what should be deleted. Each morning, the wp center checks disk space to note how quickly the memory is being used up.

Secretaries are also responsible for maintaining their own document libraries stored on floppy disks. Each secretary's directory is periodically reviewed by the system manager. If documents over two months old appear, the secretary is asked to clean up the library.

Password protection of documents is discouraged. [NBI allows discretionary use of passwords which provides a level of security for documents, as only the operator knows the password he or she entered into the system.] The in-house training program does not demonstrate the feature. The last thing we need is for someone to password protect a document, quit or forget the password! Retention of confidential documents on floppy disks kept at the secretary's desk sufficiently protects those documents. The personnel department is permitted to use the password feature, however, because of the confidential nature of their work.

Personnel Backup. Many times an attorney will bring a job to the wp center because his or her secretary is absent. A wp specialist in the center will input the document if our schedule permits. If not, it is usually handled by the personnel office which has three "floaters" who have been trained on the system. We are also training additional secretaries for back-up situations.

Results

Bottlenecks in the wp center have been reduced as a result of:

* So many secretaries having terminals;
* The ability of those who don't have terminals to have typewritten documents put on the system via OCR;
* Common access to the data base.

Our turnaround time is now reasonable and overtime has been minimized.

The implementation was not without some heartache. One of the most interesting challenges was getting attorneys and secretaries to deal with the factor of change. We realized, throughout the process, the value of patience, encouragement, a sense of humor and constant interaction.

THE SUCCESS OF SCANNING: THREE OCR USERS AND THEIR STORIES*

Government figures show that data entry represents between 30 and 50 percent of a company's information processing budget. In many instances, using optical character readers (OCRs) to replace keyboard entry of data can dramatically reduce manpower costs and improve productivity by increasing document turnaround, improving accuracy, and freeing word processing equipment to be used to full capacity. Recent technological advances have made them attractive for interfacing with a wide variety of office systems as well.

The following case histories outline the OCR experience of three different types of companies. The law firm of Arnstein, Gluck, Lehr, Barron & Milligan began with a limited OCR which it upgraded to read common type styles and interface with the firm's enhanced DP system. Home Box Office uses a sophisticated OCR with four interface ports to service its headquarters and branch offices. Golden Rule Insurance Co. uses a hand-held wand device which reads small blocks of information for tracking purposes.

A Centralized Approach

With a very small headquarters staff in New York City and a limited operating budget, the office systems group of Home Box Office (HBO) had to cope with the problem of keeping pace with the company's explosive growth. HBO, a subsidiary of Time Inc., operates two 24-hour pay TV entertainment services for millions of subscribers, who are served by over 5,000 affiliate cable TV systems throughout the United States, Puerto Rico, and the Virgin Islands.

*Republished with permission from *Office Administration and Automation*, copyright April, 1984 by Geyer-McAllister Publications, Inc., New York.

How could the office systems group possibly meet its responsibility of supporting the information processing needs of the rapidly expanding number of headquarters and branch office users?

"With our limited staff and budget, there was no way we could keep adding new terminals at each individual's desk," explains Karen Pardo, manager, office systems planning and administration. "Our philosophy was to provide a centralized approach to automating office procedures for decentralized equipment and operations. One way of doing this was to install an OCR."

After reviewing alternatives and conducting an elaborate equipment justification study, Pardo and her staff decided on an AlphaWord III+ PageReader from CompuScan, of Fairfield, N.J. The unit visually scans text that has been typed on a standard electric typewriter and instantly transmits the typed material to a word processor to be edited and formatted.

"The implementation of an OCR device instantly converted our many office typewriters into data entry terminals," Pardo adds. "It helped clear up the logjam at our terminals and boosted our overall productivity and efficiency without a corresponding heavy increase in our overhead costs."

Installed in the HBO headquarters in New York's Time and Life Building last April, the AlphaWord III+ scanner was linked to one of HBO's Wang OIS 140 Model III text editing systems. Later this year HBO will move its headquarters to a new building in midtown New York. In this new facility, the scanner will also be linked to a Wang VS 100 minicomputer which, in turn, will be linked to nine regional offices. Eventually Pardo expects to link the scanner to a Syntrex processor used by the company's legal department in New York that, in turn, is directly linked to a similar processor at its Los Angeles office.

The ability of the AlphaWord III+ PageReader to serve more than one type of processor at a time was one of the reasons HBO selected it. By loading the appropriate protocol in the scanner, it can receive text from one remote workstation and immediately forward it to a different type of workstation for editing or processing. Similarly, text from most types of computer printers can be scanned by the OCR and entered into another word or data processor for editing, further processing, or filing. These advanced features extend the operations of the OCR far beyond data entry, making it a cost-effective focal point in a company's telecommunications operations.

With 70 to 80 terminals at HBO offices across the country, many, but by no means all, managers and secretaries have access to one of the terminals. For those with limited access to terminals and extensive processing needs, the new AlphaWord III+ OCR scanner has proved to be an efficient solution. While it is most readily accessible to New York users, material from branch offices can be express-mailed to New York for immediate scanning.

"As the requests increase for additional terminals in the various HBO departments," Pardo said, "the ability to supply our users with additional terminals at reasonable cost decreases. The optical character scanner overcomes this problem by converting standard typewriters into original input equipment, thereby freeing up terminal time for high-speed editing."

In addition to turning every IBM Selectric typewriter into an original input station, the AlphaWord III+ OCR can convert any outside document into a system document, can resolve the problem of damaged diskettes by quickly scanning "hard copy," can transfer data from one unattached system to an attached system via telecommunications, and can be used by multiple departments.

Finally, substantial cost savings are realized by using the AlphaWord III+ OCR for data entry, as compared with direct keying into the Wang or Syntrex processors.

Striving for Efficiency

How do you produce over 100,000 pages of legal and administrative documents each year? To do it well, you have to balance technology and people. The people-oriented approach is used at the Chicago law firm of Arnstein, Gluck, Lehr, Barron & Milligan.

"Attorneys are independent by nature," says William O'Brien, director of administration services, "and we must serve their individual needs. We must keep the inconveniences of automation to a minimum and develop a procedure for maximum efficiency. We communicate capabilities to them and they communicate needs to us."

Founded in 1893, the law firm is one of the oldest in Chicago. With 65 attorneys occupying two floors of the Sears Tower and an office in West Palm Beach, Fla., it has almost doubled in size in the last 10 years. Some of the largest publicly owned corporations in the country are among its clients.

Timothy Seifert, manager of the word processing department, joined the firm in 1978 with the second phase of automatic document preparation, when mag cards were replaced with stand-alone text-editing machines. An OCR was attached to the word processor to facilitate the conversion. When it was completed, the word processing department contained three WP terminals, three printers, and one OCR.

The secretarial staff did most of the initial typing on IBM Selectric typewriters, and the OCR transferred the information to the WP terminals, where editing and formatting was done. Using secretaries to type first drafts meant less deciphering of handwriting and fewer decisions as to attorneys' style preferences of WP operators.

As the volume of work increased, a change had to be made. The requirements were simple: aid the attorneys in their work and provide faster processing and more professional-looking documents.

Mr. Seifert looked to OCR as a possible solution. The Hendrix Typereader 1 currently in use had restrictions—double spacing in 10-pitch only with OCR-B type style—which made documents prepared for OCR input look "different." If the restrictions could be removed, then more work would be prepared for OCR input.

The Typereader 1 was upgraded to a Typereader 2 and the best two out of three restrictions were removed.

The OCR could read single, one and a half, and double spacing in both 10- and 12-pitch. The OCR-B type style still had to be used but most of the users didn't object to that.

The firm continued to grow. A document-oriented system with both word and data processing was required. Available systems were evaluated, but there was no system that met the criteria. A major vendor provided the firm with the opportunity to Beta-test a system. The result was a system that accommodates the firm's needs.

The stand-alone text-editing machines were removed, and an integrated system was installed in their place. The Typereader 2 was upgraded to a Typereader 3, which can read common type styles, not just the OCR-B, thus eliminating the final restriction. All documents could now be entered on the system via OCR.

Mr. O'Brien stresses the need to use the capabilities of systems. Recent additions have been a streaming tape drive and an 88,000-word dictionary. These have significantly increased the ability to produce better documents faster.

A new computer system is being phased in now to expand the firm's entire data processing operation. It will handle only data processing and special-application functions. One of the future needs at Arnstein, Gluck, Lehr, Barron & Milligan will be system integration. The Typereader will be set up to enter data on both computers, and data processing applications will be added as the system expands.

Keeping Track

Each day thousands of dollars are paid out to individuals making health insurance claims. Golden Rule Insurance Company, a Lawrenceville, Illinois-based company with an executive office in Indianapolis, employs 1,000 people and receives up to 10,000 claims and 2,000 new policies per week.

In the past the company had no organized method of keeping track of all these claims and the many thousands of dollars they represent. When a policyholder or insurer called to inquire about the status of a claim, an employee would have to call around the office or hunt for the file on foot, and then call the customer back with the information, a costly, time-consuming process.

To maintain accurate records of claims and new policies and to be able to quickly trace their location and stage of completion, Golden Rule installed an automated tracking system, which uses OCR devices to track the file of each claim or new policy as it is being evaluated or issued. The system has proven so helpful to the growing company that the original installation of 12 OCR devices by Caere Corp. of Los Gatos, Calif., has been expanded to include a total of 56 devices.

"If we get a phone call from an insurer or policyholder requesting the status of a claim, we can call up the information on the computer and tell them that an adjuster is reviewing it or that we've already sent out the check," says Bob Talley, director of management information services. "The customer gets fast, accurate information, and we're able to keep accurate records. The tracking system has become the heart of our claims and policy issue business."

Golden Rule uses its computer system to print OCR-A labels, and then a clerk places a label on each file containing a new policy issuer or claim. The tracking system has two separate transaction identifications (I.D.s), one for claims and one for new policies. The employee entering the tracking information calls up the correct transaction I.D., and then passes a hand-held wand across the OCR label, thus entering the policy number and policyholder's name.

File labels are read into the tracking system with the wands twice at each department they pass through, once when they enter and once when they leave. Depending on the specifications of the policy or claim, it may pass through several departments.

"We felt an OCR tracking system using hand-held wands would be substantially more accurate than having our people try to hand-key the long policy numbers at each tracking," explains Talley.

Several individuals are designated as "communicators" for new claims and new policies. These employees handle all the incoming calls requesting information about the status of a new policy or claim. When a communicator receives a phone request for information about a claim, he or she keys in the claim transaction I.D., calling up the proper inquiry screen. Then, by typing the policyholder's name, policy number, or claim number onto a keyboard, the communicator can instantly find the current location and status of the caller's file.

Another benefit of the tracking system is that internal paperwork and mail can be easily and quickly added to a file by simply tracing the file's current location.

Golden Rule uses an IBM 4341 mainframe computer in its Lawrenceville office. The total system involves 160 terminals, with 100 used directly in the tracking. The system operates with the User Files On-line (UFO) software program by Oxford Software Co., of Hasbrouck Heights, N.J.

COPING WITH MULTI-VENDOR INSTALLATIONS*

By Paula F. Calise and Mary E. Locke

Today's multi-vendor office environment has evolved for a myriad of reasons. For example, as the variety and quality of microprocessor-driven systems increases, users are finding their presence in the office to be irresistible and indispensable. This has led to the use of many kinds of microcomputers within one organization.

This is only one of the ways multi-vendor environments are created. Some organizations choose to retain their old systems for particular applications while acquiring new generations of equipment for other applications. Whatever the reasons for their existence, multi-vendor installations are a reality many organizations will have to confront.

Some organizations choose to select obviously incompatible equipment from several vendors, while others establish an incompatible single-vendor installation by acquiring different generations of a vendor's equipment. This article looks at these two kinds of multi-vendor installations and at the obstacles and challenges management had to face.

The first company, Dynamic Development Corporation (DDC), is a progressive firm that strives to be a leader in the construction and land development field. The company employs advanced management strategies and techniques. DDC tries to reflect this progressive image in its use of word processing and makes extensive use of sophisticated word processors throughout the organization, including a dozen Xerox 860 systems, the same number of Lanier systems and a few older, IBM mag card systems.

---

*Reprinted with permission from *Words,* the *Journal of the Association of Information Systems Professionals,* August-September, 1983.

The second firm, Top North General Hospital, practices leading edge health care. A new hospital group has just been launched, and the University with whom the hospital is affiliated is internationally recognized as a hotbed for genetic research. Word processors, used for innumerable scientific and business applications, proliferate throughout the hospital. Top North utilizes a large number of IBM System 6's, and recently, Displaywriters have been placed in a number of departments. There is some talk of an IBM 5520 investigation. Top North is constantly striving to acquire state-of-the-art WP technology through a single vendor.

In the case of DDC, the different vendors are easily identifiable. Although covered up by the IBM logo, Top North reflects a multi-vendor shop with the presence of three generations of technology. Essentially, both DDC and Top North have the same word processing environment; each has a multi-vendor installation. DDC and Top North have potential opportunities and inherent problems with diverse systems in a word processing plan.

Strengths of Multi-Vendor Installations

Every system has a unique strength, performing at least one function better, quicker or easier than any of its competitors. No one feature should determine the choice of a system for an office. It is important to match a critical or dominant application to a particular system's strengths. If one vendor offers a product that best meets that critical application without forfeiting many of the other selection criteria, this equipment should be considered an excellent candidate for installation, even if it means that it will result in the introduction of a product other than an organization's chosen vendor.

An application's importance in the environment, and the general information processing strategy of the organization should be the deciding factors. There are great benefits to allowing a system best suited to an application to be installed when compatibility isn't the major criteria. One very important benefit is that matching a system's strengths with user requirements increases the probability of success.

In addition, introducing more than one vendor on a limited level can be an excellent method of testing equipment prior to general installation throughout the organization. No demonstration or reference material can provide better information for strategic systems planning than actual utilization. Vendor support, reliability, flexibility, and ease of operation can be determined in a small installation over a period of time. Introducing a second, or possibly even a third, vendor to your installation can provide an organization with invaluable information on system strengths and weaknesses.

Problems of Using Varied Equipment

Incompatibility is the most obvious problem in a multi-vendor environment and takes many forms. Unlike data processing, which acknowledges national standards, word processing has no standardization in formatting or entering information. Preformatted diskettes and varying densities make floppy disks unreadable by any system other than the one in which it originated. Beyond that, file incompatibilities exist, and systems structures differ. On some systems, commands are embedded; on others, they are not. In a multi-vendor installation, text can be passed between systems via telecommunications or converted using an OCR, but the file loses all of its encoded system commands. The document may be editable, but it is not compatible from the standpoint of formatting commands.

Another incompatibility that surfaces in a multi-vendor shop is the inability to share work loads during peak periods. Once drafted on a particular system, a document cannot be edited on a different vendor's system, even if staff utilization would make this desirable. This is particularly important when considering equipment to be used in a word processing center designed to handle overflow from various departments. Equipment choice should reflect what the document originators have selected.

In reality, however, it is virtually impossible to predict the work flow in this kind of center over a given period of time. Originators differ in their ability and capacity to produce final documents the first time through; some will require more revisions than others, and as a result, one system might be used more than another.

Incompatibility creates problems in other areas such as the training of operators and users. In addition, multiple learning curves must be developed to evaluate individuals' performance on different equipment. It also makes it more difficult for the information or word processing department to provide internal support and encourage advanced application design for various systems.

In large organizations where supply procurement is handled centrally, multi-vendor shops require supplies to be stocked in quantity, tracked and controlled. When the last printer ribbon runs out, using the surplus from another system is not always possible. The dilemma does not stop with ribbons; it extends to other supplies such as magnetic media, storage facilities and print wheels.

Multi-Vendor/Single-Vendor Strategies

In a single-vendor installation, the vendor will probably offer more assistance in integrating incompatible equipment if the contract includes a large number of systems. In the multi-vendor environment, the competitive atmosphere between vendors may help drive a more favorable deal for the user. Competing vendors keep an eye on their customers' equipment acquisitions and are quick to answer service calls. In either situation, the user organization should be aware of any bargaining position that can be used to its benefit.

An organization can dictate that there will be one vendor/product installed in all areas. As in the case of Top North Hospital, choosing a single vendor with products that are incompatible due to technology advancement will affect all the same costs of a multi-vendor shop. These costs will also be incurred when using a vendor that periodically introduces new generations of incompatible equipment.

It does not take a financial genius to recognize that it is expensive to change from a multi-vendor to a single-vendor installation. This changeover means more than simply a large financial investment in equipment. It also will create a need for retraining, media conversion, and new keyboarding procedures, and require a great number of management hours for planning and implementing this change.

The least expensive approach to bringing-about the single-vendor organization is attrition—simply letting the leases expire and replacing the systems from a single source vendor. Procedures for the new system can be installed leisurely and logically.

To soften the strict line of single-vendor/product strategy, an organization can use a service bureau to address unique applications, thus eliminating the need to address all applications. Using this approach, an organization can reap the benefits of internally consistent products, yet enjoy the added benefits of differing system strengths for unique, low-volume applications.

There are challenges ahead for companies like DDC and Top North. In both kinds of multi-vendor installations, management decisions ultimately determine success or failure. Multi-vendor strategies are both beneficial and costly to an organization. In dealing with the situation, a planned, controlled environment is important. Precautions must be taken to prevent unplanned, incompatible systems from springing up throughout an organization because of one special application. There are many positive reasons to employe the multi-vendor strategy; and, with proper planning, training and control, the probability of success will improve. More importantly, managers must know their system's strengths, and work hard to avoid the pitfalls of incompatibility.

OFFICE AUTOMATION: WHO'S IN CONTROL?*

By Paula F. Calise and Mary Locke

Converging technologies in data and word processing, voice and data communications, electronic mail and other areas are bringing us capabilities only dreamed of a few years ago. However, new administrative dilemmas and challenges are arising. These must be met by management soon or the advantages promised by office automation (OA) will be lost in a corporate tug-of-war.

Consider a typical, but fictitious, company, Successful Corp. This is a mature organization whose market share, even during the recession, did not dwindle. The firm employs advanced management practices in the administration of its manufacturing, marketing, employee relations and most other functional areas. Top management is proud of its financial record, and so are its stockholders.

Also, over the past 15 years or so, the company has committed to keeping abreast of the benefits that can be reaped from a strong data processing (DP) development strategy. Recently, a separate office for the development of advanced office technology, called advanced office services, was established and supported generously with funds for pilot projects and numerous office automation installations.

The president of the company has chartered the vice president of administration and the vice president of finance with jobs that together will move Successful into the information age. The vice president of administration's responsibility is to provide all levels of the organization with the support tools and training they need to disseminate, access and retrieve automated organizational information.

The vice president of finance's organization will provide the technological tools, as well as the generation and storage of the data. Since there will be a single source of organization information, no duplication by the various organizational entities should be tolerated.

The finance vice president, over a period of time, has developed a strong data processing organization. The department is quite efficient in its operation, and single-source data suits them fine. No multi-generations and revisions of data need to be maintained. A mainframe computer is used in conjunction with various peripherals to create an up-to-date hop. Recently, the department began to disseminate processing power throughout the organization, with personal computers (PCs) provided to many divisional and departmental managers.

Linking PCs

These PCs are linked via telecommunications to the database on the mainframe, and more applications and telecommunications interfaces are being used by these managers. The vice president of finance's most recent, and most far-reaching, announcement is that the data processing department will soon implement an organization-wide network, which will include remote sites, encompassing a wide breadth of communications facilities. Obviously, this department is on top of technology and data management.

The vice president of administration has a number of accomplishments to be proud of as well. The department has successfully installed a computerized administrative system, and placed this system on the desks of most administrative secretaries, and some production secretaries, throughout the organization. Plans have been completed to expand the system to remote locations, tying the system together through telecommunications. Software, soon to be installed on the mainframe, will allow the administrative system to use the mainframe for mass storage, among other things. The administrative system is heavily used for word processing, and an electronic mail capability is becoming increasingly popular for intraoffice correspondence.

System Authority

Recently, Successful became interested in "hanging" personal computers, set up by the DP department, on the administrative system, set up by advanced office services. When a PC emulates the administrative system, using its resources, whose system is it? Who troubleshoots? Who assists the user? Who recovers any lost information?

Further, when the administrative system, through the use of special-purpose software, taps into the mainframe, does that make the screen a mainframe terminal under the domain of data processing, or will the user call advanced office services for assistance in problem solving? Also, the large network that data processing intends to install is designed, among other things, to handle text applications. But it is the administrative system that will be the source of that type of transmission. Who "owns" the interface and communication authority in this case?

The stage is set at Successful Corporation for untold instances of miscommunication, unclear domain problems, confused and frustrated users, and ultimately an ongoing game of finger pointing. The line of authority is blurring as to which division "owns" the systems, including the problems, solutions and application development. The mud puddle is built, the rope is strung, and the corporate tug-of-war is about to begin.

MIS and WP

Many organizations find themselves with two separate reporting lines for traditional data processing (called management information systems in many organizations) and word processing [information processing] (office systems). The problem is that the technologies are converging, even becoming entwined. It is becoming increasingly unclear which systems, applications, training and trouble-shooting responsibilities lie where. Two groups within the same organization are eagerly attempting to encourage the use of "their" systems.

There is no longer, today, a clear line between data processing and word processing functions. Any personal computer can add word processing software, and most word processors allow the use of some accounting or spreadsheet (DP) functions. Now add the need to communicate between dissimilar devices, or to the mainframe, and the puzzle becomes even more complicated.

Some organizations have further complicated the picture by involving a third department: the data processing department is responsible for its function, the word processing department is chartered with its responsibilities, and a communications department claims responsibility for the cable and software that tie together data processing and word processing devices.

The tug-of-war over the use of information systems is in full swing at Successful. The functional divisions involved are vying for predominance in two ways. First, each group is sending staff into various departments identifying potential applications for its systems. And second, there is an absolutely hectic attempt by both data processing and advanced office services to place as many of "their" screens as possible.

The user is in the middle. Where does the user look for objective application design assistance, orientation, installation assistance, and preliminary and advanced training? The same end user, the middle manager in most cases, needs both technologies but cannot await the winner of the tug-of-war. However, the manager cannot proceed with installations since the ultimate victor is not evident.

The costs involved in this tug-of-war are high. Each division, data processing and advanced office services, views the other with a degree of mistrust. Each knows that the other does not truly understand its position, technology, and rapport with users. And chances are, this problem is exacerbated because the two groups do not even speak the same language. The lexicon of traditional data processing and office automation is very different. The impending mistrust and suspicion between the divisions makes the growth of a cooperative environment difficult, if not impossible.

Territorial Attitudes

The lack of cross-training of information department staff members, due to this territorial attitude, costs the organization a great deal, too. Often, both financial areas are working toward common goals, or solving like problems, but are doing so separately. The cost of the two organizations' resources being devoted to the solution of one problem is simply too expensive and wasteful, particularly since the solutions are likely to be divergent rather than parallel. The two divisions begin a subtle competition for users and for the organization's attention and resources.

What can Successful do to avoid this fate? One strategy is to bring both legs of its information resources together under the control of a single vice president. Initially, the more likely candidate would be the vice president of finance, since the bulk of the computer horsepower lies within this division.

But a look at the evolutionary changes taking place in the use of information resources brings to light a different solution. The trend in information resource use lies more in support of managers using decision support systems. Managers will increasingly become the predominant users of organizational information for all types of work and decision making. This being the case, designing and employing user training, customized application design and implementation assistance will ultimately become the bulk of the work required by information staff members. With this perspective, it may be that the skills the vice president of administration's staff possesses are more in line with future demands of the information environment. The control of all information resources would reside under his or her administration.

A third possibility is for the president of the company to consider creating a top-management position whose total responsibility is information support and management. This could very well be the best solution for Successful because, under a vice president of its own, information resources would be guaranteed the attention it deserves.

The selection of any of the above choices, although it is likely to be politically painful, could result in a solution to the tug-of-war dilemma. Under a single vice president's domain, ownership of systems would not be an issue, the user could identify one source of support, a single solution to problems would develop, and a healthy, less competitive environment would result. The political pain incurred in moving toward unified information resource management would be only short term. The long-term injury to the organization of allowing the tug-of-war to continue would be much more substantial.

These problems are present in most organizations today. They call for corporate attention to provide creative solutions. It is time to declare a truce in the tug-of-war, and to define and construct the peace.

PROFILE: THE WORD/INFORMATION PROCESSING MANAGER*

By Jean Green Dorsey

A type of manager who didn't exist 15 years ago is now responsible for changing many of the operations, methods and procedures of today's office. This executive carries out a number of management roles and often heads a large department. In addition, the rapid advances in the integration of office systems, such as word and data processing, have created a need for a manager who can coordinate a number of diverse technologies.

The word/information processing (W/IP) manager is that coordinator. He or she is responsible for improving support to management by providing instant access to information resources, increasing office productivity, selecting and operating advanced office systems, and achieving cost savings.

As a result, the W/IP manager must be able to work effectively with clerical and professional personnel and report to a variety of second- and third-level managers (vice presidents of administration, MIS directors, controllers and the like).

Though lumped under the umbrella designation of information manager, these people have a variety of titles. Some of the more widely used are: manager, office planning and services; director, information systems; administrative director; vice president, MIS; and office administrator.

The sudden and relatively recent development of information management as a profession is underscored by the International Information/Word Processing (IWP) [author's note: this organization has changed its name to Association of

---

*Reprinted with permission from *Today's Office*, June 1982, Hearst Business Publications, Inc.

Information Systems Professionals (AISP)] survey on job tenure, which reveals that 77 percent of the information managers questioned have had their positions for less than four years. Furthermore, according to the association, information managers are a young group: 77 percent are 45 years old or younger, with a majority of them falling into the 26- to 35-year-old category.

Where are these trailblazers coming from? What are their backgrounds and qualifications? As varied as the responsibilities of the job.

Today's group of W/IP supervisors comprises high-school graduates who joined their organizations as beginning secretaries, college graduates with liberal arts degrees and people with backgrounds in business education.

At first glance, it would appear that these supervisors were in the right place at the right time. However, as is usually the case, there was more to it than that: these workers saw an opportunity, possessed initiative and foresight, and developed impressive on-the-job track records.

Many W/IP supervisors began as secretaries and word processing operators. This was the case with Mary Jane Ornelas Walter, manager of the secretarial support unit at Eastern Airlines in Miami. She was the first in her company to begin using word processing to handle the high volume of customer form letters that had to be produced.

Ornelas Walter started her WP career in 1966, and today has responsibility for office automation, which includes administrative support, phones, and mail and filing systems. She heads a staff of 70 people, including word processing, secretarial and administrative personnel.

Theresa Wingerter, manager of word and data processing for Liskow & Lewis, a New Orleans law firm, had a background as an executive secretary and made the jump to management when she convinced the firm to utilize word processors. She was given responsibility for the project—planning to implementation.

Wingerter now supervises all word and data processing personnel. Her primary responsibility is to determine the applications for all OA equipment and ensure full utilization.

A secretarial background can be very useful to the word

and information processing supervisor. For one thing, it means that the individual possesses the facility to handle all manner of office equipment.

Hands-on experience with office equipment is also likely to result in a more empathetic approach towards machine operators. By displaying the necessary machine skills and demonstrating willingness to learn how new equipment works, the manager makes it easier to gain employee acceptance of new office systems.

"It is essential that a supervisor be able to handle the office equipment, whether she actually does or not," says Linda K. Popp, word processing supervisor at Deere & Company in Moline, Illinois.

Dave Palagi, a word processing supervisor who was promoted to methods analyst at Commonwealth Edison Company, Chicago, agrees. "It is important for the supervisor to be really involved with the equipment," he says. "This way, you know all the things it can do; you can find the applications and apply them."

Although many of the women supervisors interviewed rose from the secretarial ranks, the men generally came from more diverse backgrounds. For instance, David Slagle had worked as an editor and was getting his Master's degree in psychology when his employment agency suggested he consider a career in word processing. He subsequently became the word processing manager at Price Waterhouse, Washington, D.C. After two years, he was promoted to office automation specialist.

Neither did Dennis Darr have any experience in word processing when he became the supervisor of the WP center at American Telephone & Telegraph in San Francisco. Prior to that position, he had been the supervisor of an AT&T methods-and-procedures unit. In that job, Darr wrote standards manuals and office-procedures handbooks.

Darr cultivated his WP skills at company training sessions, aimed for the most part at people who were self-trained, and through various seminars.

Dean Plummer, currently the director of WP Management Changes for New York's Department of General Services, is another self-taught WP manager. "I learned on the job," he readily admits.

Plummer's background doesn't fit the standard W/IP mold: urban studies degree, experience as a political organizer and consultant after college, stint as a production manager for a magazine, some graphics experience. But Plummer says his political background has been very valuable, because so much of his job involves making policy and personnel decisons.

In a field where today's newest processing marvel can be next month's relic, W/IP supervisors are constantly investigating the latest technology, while at the same time, fine-tuning their applications and management skills. The IWP reports that the W/IP supervisor is usually in charge of four or more office technologies, generally including WP, telecommunications, electronic mail, data processing, reprographics, phototypesetting and data-base management.

Knowledge of office technology is essential, but it is not the only skill needed by today's W/IP supervisor. "Management skills are increasingly important to information managers," says Bernard Schwartz, director of communication for IWP. "They feel that it has become as vital to their jobs as understanding the equipment and procedures."

In fact, the IWP-survey respondents rated supervisory skills and management techniques as third and fifth in importance, respectively, in a listing of job qualifications.

It is interesting that a position dependent on machinery and automation should emphasize the human element as much as that of W/IP management. Even those managers who feel that they "fell into word processing" talk about a humanistic approach to their jobs, their supervisors and their subordinates.

The right blend of shrewd bottom-line management and a real understanding of personnel considerations can result in maximum productivity, according to Dee Mitchell, director of word processing for Blue Cross/Blue Shield Associations in Chicago. Mitchell stresses good personnel relations, and her efforts in this regard have been innovative and successful.

With her three supervisors, Mitchell instituted the hiring of high-school students for part-time work. The students are trained, perform "real" work and are encouraged to join the firm upon graduation. They are, she says proudly, almost immediately productive.

Dee Mitchell also exemplifies the W/IP manager's emphasis on cost justification. Her superiors rely on her judgement for progressive equipment changes and staffing, as long as it is cost justified. Her center has tracked costs since the initial startup, and Mitchell happily reports a 199 percent increase in productivity and a 48 percent reduction in per-page costs.

In order to maintain the highest departmental efficiency and productivity, today's W/IP supervisors must keep abreast of the newest products, procedures and techniques. To do this, supervisors attend conventions and seminars on upcoming products and trends, as well as college courses on business and management. They read extensively and meet with product vendors and other supervisors to discuss the latest approaches and ideas for processing information.

There is, of course, still a way to go. W/IP managers feel they have certain obstacles to overcome before they can perform at top efficiency. Those responding to the IWP survey spoke of the stress associated with deadline pressures and decried the lack of clarity regarding information processing's role in the corporate hierarchy. Other sources of occupational growing pains were the rapidity of change in the industry and an ignorance about information processing on the part of top management.

Today's word and information processing manager is filling a very demanding spot—one that is increasingly important to the corporation, as office systems play an ever-larger role in increasing operator efficiency. As a result of their experiences in this area, W/IP managers are moving up the corporate ladder and into other areas of the company.

Barbara Rodriguez, director of communication services at Arthur Young and Company, New York, typifies the trend toward corporate management and consulting. "The most important thing," Rodriguez says, "is to know what your organization's style of doing things is. Too many people think they only have to know what the equipment can do, but you have to join the management team and concentrate on being a manager, not a technologist."

Upper-level managers, recognizing the vaue and transferability of the W/IP supervisor's communication and persuasion proficiencies, often consider them candidates for management-development and human-resources training staff positions. As one W/IP supervisor maintains, if you combine management skills with the proper technical background, your career horizons can be unlimited.

The word and information processing manager is no longer a novice but still faces the quite substantial challenge of creating a quality work environment with the best of both people and technological resources. Sailing through these relatively uncharted waters can be hazardous, but the rewards are often worth it: limitless growth potential and career satisfaction.

BIBLIOGRAPHY

Bennetts, Keith. "LAN Firm: PBX Makers Still Playing Catch Up." *MIS Week,* 9 May 1984.

"Boeing Offers CPU Training." *MIS Week,* 9 May 1984.

Bohl, Marilyn. *Information Processing,* 4th ed. Chicago: Science Research Associates, Inc., 1984.

Calise, Paula F., & Mary E. Locke, "Coping with Multivendor Installations." *Words, the Journal of the Association of Information Systems Professionals,* Aug.-Sept., 1983. p. 34–36.

Cowan, William M., "The, 'I Center'—An Office Resource Comes of Age." *Office Administration and Automation,* February 1984, p. 30–31, 51.

"Dial-up for Fast Stock Quotes." *MIS Week,* 30 May, 1984.

Dickinson, John. "IBM's Display Writer Begets a Family of PC Software" *PC Magazine,* 18 September, 1984, p. 240–241.

Dolecheck, Carolyln Crawford, & Danny W. Murphy. *Applied Word Processing: An Introduction to Text Editing with Keyboarding Applications.* Dallas, Texas: South-Western Publishing Co., 1983.

Dooley, Bill. "Lowell's Tots Getting CPUs." *MIS Week,* 4 April 1984, p. 32.

Dooley, Bill. "Typewriter That 'Hears' Lures Wang." *MIS Week,* 3 October, 1984.

Dooley, Bill. "Venture a Boost for Videotex." *MIS Week,* 25 April 1984, p. 34.

Egan, Mike. "Firestone: Implementing a Micro Strategy." *Micro Manager,* Supplement to *MIS Week,* April 1984, p. 11.

"Educating the User: The Next Challenge." *Words,* April-May, 1984, p. 20–39.

"Extraordinary Communications at the Olympics." *Office Administration and Automation,* June 1984, p. 62–63.

History of Computer Systems, Sperry, n.d., n.p.

"Houston U, DEC Join In Project." *MIS Week,* 13 June 1984, p. 6.

"Improving the Quality of Light . . . and Work Performance." *Office Administration and Automation,* May, 1984, p. 39–40.

Letter received from Ratheon Data Systems Company. Norwood, MA, 27 Feb. 1984.

Locke, Mary E., & Paula Calise, "Taking Control of Automation." *Management World,* October 1983, p. 18–20.

Minicucci, Rick. "West Coast Group Brings OA Down to Earth." *Today's Office,* June 1982, p. 29.

Polilli, Steve. "Playnet Offers National Fun On-Line." *MIS Week,* 14 November 1984, p. 54.

Rosen, Jo Ann. "Proofreading Skills Reflect Quality Performance," *Words,* December-January 1984, p. 36–38.

Schwartz, Lloyd. "Agency: Little Ground for VDT Health Perils." *MIS Week,* 23 May 1984, p. 22.

"Standalone Word Processing Systems." *Datapro Research Reports,* January, 1978.

Syncom's Product Manual. Syncom®, Mitchell, SD. Section 2, pp. 1–11.

The Directory of Office Information Systems: Reference and Buyer's Guide. 2nd ed. New York, NY: Published for the Association of Information Systems Professionals by Information Clearing House, 1983.

The Seybold Report on Office Systems. Published by Seybold Publications, Inc. Media, PA: 1 January 1985, p. 17.

Tregoboff, Dan. "ABA Says CPU Crime Rampant." *MIS Week,* 20 June 1984, p. 6.

"Video terminal awareness: Westminister students like required computer course." *The Daily Sentinel,* Grand Junction, CO., 2 November, 1983, p. 5.

"Wall Street Journal Goes On-Line." *MIS Week,* 30 May, 1984.

Williams, Bryan. "Office Systems Standards Are Going Forward." *MIS Week,* Feb. 22, 1984.

1982 Annual Report, Northern Telecom Limited, p. 26.

Index